Home Office Research Study 192

Explaining reconviction following a community sentence: the role of social factors

by
Chris May

**A Research, Development and
Statistics Directorate Report**

London: Home Office

Home Office Research Studies

The Home Office Research Studies are reports on research undertaken by or on behalf of the Home Office. They cover the range of subjects for which the Home Secretary has responsibility. Titles in the series are listed at the back of this report (copies are available from the address on the back cover). Other publications produced by the Research, Development and Statistics Directorate include Research Findings, the Research Bulletin, Statistical Bulletins and Statistical Papers.

The Research, Development and Statistics Directorate

The Research, Development and Statistics Directorate is an integral part of the Home Office, serving the Ministers and the department itself, its services, Parliament and the public through research, development and statistics. Information and knowledge from these sources informs policy development and the management of programmes; their dissemination improves wider public understanding of matters of Home Office concern.

First published 1999

Application for reproduction should be made to the Information and Publications Group, Room 201, Home Office, 50 Queen Anne's Gate, London SW1H 9AT.

©Crown copyright 1999 ISBN 1 84082 219 8
ISSN 0072 6435

Foreword

Over the last five years, the Offenders and Correction Unit has produced a number of research and statistical studies about predicting reconviction; it has developed a number of algorithms for use by practitioners to estimate probabilities of reconviction; and it has examined the impact of probation and prison programmes by comparing actual and predicted reconviction rates. Most of that work has concentrated on the role of criminal history variables in predicting reconviction.

This report describes the results of the first large-scale British study to investigate the link between social factors and reconviction for offenders serving community sentences. The results of the study suggest that probation work with offenders in tackling problems chiefly with drugs, but also with employment, accommodation and finances, may play a role in reducing offending. The report underlines the case for a much wider range of factors to be recorded routinely by probation services and for a single approach to recording to be adopted nationally.

CHRIS LEWIS
Head of the Offenders and Corrections Unit

Acknowledgements

I would like to thank the following Home Office colleagues for their help in formulating the research or in commenting on drafts of this report: Peter Goldblatt, Elliot Grant, Carol Hedderman, Chris Kershaw, Chris Lewis, Natalie Aye Maung and Julie Vennard. Carol Hedderman in particular guided the research from an early stage. Joanne Goodman and Quyen Luong assisted Chris Kershaw in providing reconviction data from the Offenders Index.

I am grateful to John Kay of Nottinghamshire Probation Service for first offering data for the study and pointing out the availability of information on social factors in probation areas.

Special thanks go to the Chief Probation Officers of the six areas which gave us access to their data and to the technical staff who provided the data.

Finally I would like to thank Professor Peter Raynor of the University of Wales, Swansea for his helpful comments on an earlier draft.

CHRIS MAY

Contents

	Page
Foreword	**iii**
Acknowledgements	**iv**
Summary	**vii**

1	**Introduction**	**1**
	Previous research	2
	The current study	3
	The structure of the report	4

2	**Methodology and data**	**5**
	Methodology	5
	The data	5
	The definition of 'social' factor	6
	Significance testing	7
	Pseudo-reconvictions	7

3	**The association of criminal history variables with reconviction**	**9**
	Area and disposal	9
	Age and sex	10
	Previous convictions	10
	Previous custodial sentences	12
	Rate of acquiring previous guilty appearances	12
	Offence	13

4	**The social variables covered in the study**	**15**
	Accommodation	16
	Employment	17
	Alcohol	18
	Drugs	18
	Financial problems	19
	Other social variables	20
	The variation of reconviction with different combinations of social factors	20
	Relationships between social factors and criminal history variables	21
	Summary of this chapter	26

5 The use of social variables to improve prediction   **27**
Interactions between the predictor variables   28
The multivariate analyses   32
The effect of social factors on predicting reconviction early
    in criminal careers   37
The effect of sentence   38

6 Differences in reconviction rates between areas   **45**
Implications for predicting reconviction   47

7 Conclusions   **49**

**Appendix A   Details of the social variables available for
each area**   **51**

Appendix B   Details of the logistic regressions   **52**

Appendix C   Interaction groups   **58**

References   **61**

Summary

Most research into reconviction and statistical tools to predict reconviction has focused on criminal history variables such as the number of previous convictions and the nature of the current offence. This is partly because such variables are routinely held on national statistical databases, whereas information about social characteristics is limited to a few 'static' factors such as sex and date of birth. Such data are central to predicting future behaviour, and offer useful background information for probation staff when beginning to assess offenders' needs and the risks they pose. However, in deciding how to work with an offender to reduce reoffending officers need to know which 'dynamic' factors, for example being unemployed or taking drugs, are related to offending.

This study of those sentenced to community penalties examines the additional influence that a range of social factors may have on reconviction rates. The study used data from 1993 on more than 7,000 offenders from six probation services to examine reconvictions within two years of commencement of a community penalty. It is important to appreciate that the study is restricted to a consideration of the factors these services routinely collected: it does not claim to cover comprehensively every social factor that might be related to reconviction.

The variation of reconviction rates with criminal history variables

The data were first examined to confirm that previously known relationships with reconviction still held. It was found that reconviction rates were lower for community service than for probation, but also varied across areas. On average, reconviction was lower for females and older offenders. There was a steep rise in the reconviction rate from those with no previous guilty appearances to those with about seven. Females on average had lower numbers of previous guilty appearances than males; however, for a given number of previous appearances their rate of reconviction was similar. The reconviction rate is on average higher for offenders with a history of previous convictions and custody. Reconviction rates were lower for sex offenders and higher for burglars. These findings are generally in line with previous research.

The social variables covered in the study

Information was available for each of the six study areas on five social variables: accommodation, employment, alcohol, drugs and finance. The coding systems used by areas differed, and the level of recording of variables differed over areas. Possibly, those services with particular programmes could have been more proactive in seeking out information on relevant factors. The resulting area differences in the data available will have affected the findings. However, the study shows:

- Drug use was highly related to reconviction in all areas.

- A significant relationship between the use of alcohol and reconviction was apparent in one area only.

- Employment variables were significantly related to reconviction rates in each of the areas, and this result confirms the relationship found in other studies.

- Accommodation was related to reconviction – those with problems were more likely to be reconvicted. Where no difference was apparent the numbers involved were small.

- There was evidence in some, but not all, of the six areas of a simple relationship between financial problems and reconviction.

- Offenders with multiple problems were more likely to be reconvicted.

- Some groups of offenders with particular combinations of age group and numbers of previous guilty appearances (and in some cases social factors) had significantly high or low rates of reconviction.

Information was available for other social factors in only some of the six study areas. However, although the results are based on smaller numbers, some of these factors were related to reconviction at a statistically significant level, including:

- peer group pressure;

- problems with relationships;

- being a past victim of violence.

The reconviction rates for single offenders and those with partners were virtually identical, and there was no indication that having dependent children affected reconviction. Neither physical nor mental health was correlated with reconviction in any of the areas recording these variables.

Social variables and prediction

A statistical technique (logistic regression) was used to study the relationship with reconviction of several factors taken together. The first such analyses included *only* the criminal history variables to form a basis against which to test the addition of the social variables. The most significant criminal history variable for each area was the rate of acquiring previous court appearances resulting in a conviction. Next in significance was current age. Sex was not significantly associated with reconviction in this analysis. Two offences – burglary and theft & handling – were significant in the analysis covering all six areas; both were associated with generally higher reconviction rates than other offences.

The second set of analyses examined the improvement in predictive power arising when social variables were added. For each separate probation area their addition increased the predictive power slightly. Problems with drugs, employment and finances were each significant for four areas out of the six, either by themselves or in combination with other variables. The most significant of these was drug misuse. Accommodation problems were associated with higher reconviction levels in only one area model. None of the variables unique to an area reached significance in the analyses.

The results indicate that social variables are significantly related to reconviction but that their effect in improving prediction is only slight. This is because the relationship of reconviction with criminal history factors is so strong. It is possible that the effect of social variables would have been increased had there been more consistent coding of the social variables across areas.

There was evidence that the effect on prediction of social variables was greater for less experienced offenders, that is those with fewer than three previous guilty appearances. Predictors including social factors are therefore likely to be especially useful for offenders with little criminal history on which to base an assessment.

Reconviction for different community penalties

Reconviction rates for different community penalties were compared. Offenders on probation orders with added requirements tended to exhibit high risk characteristics, whilst those on community service had lower proportions of the risk factors. For example, fewer of those on community service had large numbers of previous appearances, or had served youth custody. This pattern of the occurrence of risk factors was consistent with the pattern of reconvictions for different community sentences.

It was found that the choice of disposal was significantly affected by social factors, generally more so than by criminal history. For example, males for whom no social problems were recorded had a greatly increased chance of being selected for community service compared with other offenders.

Prediction results for one area and for all six areas taken together were improved by taking into account whether the sentence was community service. In other words, the low reconviction rate for this sentence could not entirely be explained by the criminal history and available social factors of offenders. This suggests that the sentence itself may have had a positive effect on reconviction.

Differences in reconviction rates between areas

There were considerable differences between the reconviction rates of the six areas in the study. For straight probation, no simple relationships could be discerned between offenders' characteristics and the differences in reconviction rates across areas. For community service, there were significant differences. However, the differences in reconviction between areas could not be entirely accounted for by a statistical model that included offender characteristics and type of community sentence. The area differences may be explained by social factors not available for analysis, or by differences in local factors such as police clear-up rates or differences in probation programmes.

Conclusions

The results of the study suggest that probation work with offenders in tackling problems chiefly with drugs, but also with employment, accommodation and finances, may play a role in reducing offending. The nature of the link between reconviction and problems with alcohol is less clear. Further work on this and on other dynamic social factors is needed before clear policy recommendations can be made on them.

With consistent coding, social factors could make a useful contribution to prediction methods by improving the prediction for certain classes of offender, such as drug misusers and the homeless. A knowledge of social factors could, in particular, improve prediction for cases with little criminal history.

The coding of social variables should include both objective and subjective elements. For example, accommodation should have both a factual code (such as 'home-owner', 'council rent', 'private rent' and so on) and an informed assessment as to whether an offender's accommodation is a problem that could affect offending. The former would give valuable demographic information, while the latter would make the best contribution to risk assessment. Future work on defining and coding social factors should extend beyond the five main ones covered in this study, to include other potentially predictive factors such as peer group pressure and problems with relationships. A data collection and coding system for national use would ideally be able to supply information needed locally, and would also need to be integrated with risk and needs assessment.

The study found that social factors affected the choice of disposal for those given a community penalty. Therefore, while the use of social factors in prediction may be limited, they could potentially be very important in future studies of sentencing decisions and in targeting probation programmes.

Social variables should be collected both at the start of an order and at its termination to improve prediction and to help determine the effect of supervision.

The detail of the changes to be made to the current predictors to incorporate social factors must await the outcome of future research based on more consistent data. This should enable the differences in reconviction rates between areas and between disposal groups to be better understood. Also, to allow comparison of community penalties and custody, the collection of social data on prisoners and on those serving community penalties should be aligned.

1 Introduction

The ability to assess an offender's likelihood of reoffending is central to the work of the probation service. It is a key consideration when advising courts through pre-sentence reports about what type of sentence might be most suitable, when devising a supervision plan for those given a community sentence or being released from prison, and when subsequently carrying out that supervision. Yet two or three years ago a number of reports showed that this was not something the probation service as a whole was doing well (Burnett, 1996; HMI Probation, 1995).

In response, the Home Office, the Association of Chief Officers of Probation (ACOP) and individual services took a number of steps, including:

- developing the Offender Group Reconviction Scale (OGRS) which is an actuarial scale, based primarily on criminal history variables, for predicting reconviction within two years (see Copas, 1998);

- publishing a review of the available research on the assessment and management of risk and dangerousness (Kemshall, 1996);

- commissioning a study of the benefits of three different assessment scales (Aubrey and Hough, 1997);

- producing a joint Home Office/ACOP guide to assessing and managing dangerous offenders (1997); and, most recently,

- publishing a guide to managing effective supervision (HMI, 1998).

The research described in this report is also part of this programme of work. It focuses on a key question which underlies much of the other work but which is rarely addressed directly – what role do social factors play in reconviction and how much do they add to predicting reconviction over and above criminal history variables?

Previous research

There is now a large and growing body of international literature on predicting reconviction (Chapter 5 of Kemshall (1996) and Chapter 8 of Goldblatt and Lewis (1998) give useful references). Reviewing the most recent United Kingdom studies leads to the following main conclusions.

- Previous national studies of reconviction, such as that by Lloyd et al (1994), have concentrated on factors available on statistical databases, such as age, sex and some aspects of current and previous offending. These predictive models vary in how their components are defined, but most are similar to OGRS which is calculated from an offender's number of previous convictions, age at sentence, type of offence, sex, age at first offence, rate at which the offender has acquired convictions and number of previous custodial sentences while under 21.

- The concentration on criminal history variables is partly attributable to their predictive power, but also reflects the fact that it is much easier to obtain this information. No consistent national information on other 'social' factors is currently available.

- Prediction scales based on criminal history variables are usually quite accurate. However, an offender's criminal history cannot be changed, so such scales do not help probation officers to identify and change dynamic factors which may be linked with reoffending.

- Social factors have figured in previous studies, for example in work by Ward (1987), Merrington (1990), Humphrey, Carter and Pease (1991) and Copas, Marshall and Tarling (1996). These studies looked at criminal history and some social variables, mainly focusing on employment and marital status and accommodation factors. However, definitions of these factors varied from one study to another and no clear picture emerges on whether any one is influential or whether they improve predictions based on criminal history variables.

- Predictive models of reconviction are increasingly used to assess the effect of different types of community penalties (for example, Kershaw, 1997), but it is not clear how far differences in reconviction rates relate to social factors as opposed to criminal history.

The need for the current study is clear. Lloyd, Mair and Hough (1994), recognised that a shortcoming of their study was that it could not examine the relative contribution of social variables in predicting reconviction. In addition, recent (unpublished) Home Office studies on offenders who had been dealt with by means of a fine and on paroled prisoners, have suggested that social variables may help to explain reconviction patterns.

The current study

The research described in this report aims to reduce this gap in our knowledge by examining what additional influence, if any, social factors have on the prediction of reconviction for those sentenced to community penalties. In particular, it focuses on the following questions.

- What do social factors add to existing models for predicting reconviction?

- Does the type of sentence imposed affect reconviction rates?

- Are the differences in reconviction rates between probation areas a reflection of differences in the characteristics of offenders given particular disposals, or something more?

In the course of answering these questions the study throws light on variations in the method and extent of the recording of social factors in different areas. It also considers whether the results of the study could be used to improve the reliability of prediction scores or to refine the probation service's assessment of where intervention could be beneficial.

The study is particularly timely given that many probation services are investing in assessment scales such as LSI-R (Andrews and Bonta, 1995) and the ACE system (developed by the Probation Studies Unit and Warwickshire Probation Service). These include static social factors (such as sex) and dynamic social factors (such as education or drug misuse) as well as criminal history variables.

In considering the results it is important to bear in mind that, after carrying out a feasibility study to check the sort of data probation areas held on social factors, a decision was taken to pursue this research retrospectively rather than prospectively. In other words, it was decided that this study should be based on information that was routinely held by a number of different probation services about offenders commencing supervision in 1993. The alternative would have been to invest in a huge and very expensive data collection exercise on new cases and then allow at least three years to elapse before examining reconvictions. The retrospective method allowed the research to be completed in 18 months, but did have disadvantages. Firstly, probation services do not collect information on all social factors, nor even on all which might be related to reoffending. They are selective for a variety of historical and practical reasons and are guided by professional beliefs. This may mean that the study has missed potentially influential factors. Secondly, it was not possible to specify which aspects of a factor were recorded. For these reasons it is important to see this research not as a comprehensive investigation of the influence of every social factor on reconviction but as a study of the relationship between the social information that some probation services collect and the reconvictions of offenders subject to community sentences.

It should also be recognised that this research does not reveal the *mechanism* of any link between social or other factors and reconviction. For example, although the research shows that there is a relationship between drug misuse and reconviction, it is not possible to use this in isolation as the basis for an argument that drug misuse *causes* crime. Similarly, the research does not show that tackling drug misuse will necessarily reduce crime. However, it may be intuitively clear that there is some truth in these assertions, and it may be confirmed by other research – see, for example, Edmunds (1998) on the link between reducing drug misuse and burglary. Such research is important in determining which social problems can lead to crime and therefore need to be addressed by probation services and other agencies as part of a strategy to reduce offending.

The structure of the report

Chapter 2 gives details of the methodology and the size and composition of the data sample. Chapter 3 shows the results of simple correlations of criminal history factors with reconviction. Chapter 4 describes the availability of social factors for the study and gives simple correlations with reconviction. Chapter 5 looks at which of these relationships is sustained once the impact of other factors is taken into account. This chapter also discusses the effect of disposal. Chapter 6 examines the differences in reconviction rates between probation areas. The report concludes in Chapter 7 by discussing the overall results and the implications arising from the study.

2 Methodology and data

Methodology

The study follows the methodology used by Lloyd et al (1994), concentrating on reconvictions within two years of commencement of a community penalty. Reconviction data were drawn from the Home Office Offenders Index (OI), which is a national database comprising information on all Standard List convictions since 1963 (from which the less serious summary offences are excluded). The final sample consists of those offenders who could be found on the OI and who had a Standard List offence before starting supervision, or whose supervision was itself for a Standard List offence.

Social variables are not routinely recorded by all probation areas, so Chief Probation Officers were asked for access to any data they held which would be suitable for the study. Thirty of the (then) 55 areas were in principle willing to offer data. The responses were tested against the following criteria: the period covered, the stages at which data were recorded, the variables available and their method of coding.

Eight areas were chosen which best satisfied these criteria. In the event, six of these areas supplied data on commencements in 1993. Originally it was planned to use data for 1994 also, but at the time the analysis was begun 1994 OI data for matching were not available.

The data

Table 2.1 shows the sample sizes of the datasets provided by the areas and of the matched sample by disposal group, that is probation, community service order (CSO) and combination order (a court order combining probation and community service). The left-hand column gives the potential sample – the number of persons commencing orders in 1993. The second column is the number of cases supplied by each area, and the third is the number of these that were matched with OI information. In some cases the number supplied by an area is higher than the number of commencements; it is possible that in 1993 some cases did not find their way onto the Probation Index, which collates numbers of commencements[1].

---

1   A probation service's share of resources now depends partly on its recorded caseload. This may act as an inducement to ensure that full information is passed to the Probation Index.

A high percentage of matched cases was found for nearly all areas and disposals; overall, the final number of probation and CSO cases was about 80 per cent of potential cases. The percentage matched was low only for probation orders in Dorset, of which only 56 per cent of cases supplied could be matched with the OI. Further examination of the lost cases shows that the loss was especially high for probation orders with Day Centre[2] as an added requirement. This could in part arise from Day Centre orders being made on offenders who were not convicted for Standard List offences; for example, drunk driving was not a Standard List offence at that time. The final sample for Dorset is nevertheless of a reasonable size. Table 3.1 in the next chapter shows that the reconviction rate for the Dorset sample closely matches that for cases on the OI, indicating that no obvious bias has been introduced by the loss of cases.

The figures in the first three columns of Table 2.1 are based on orders rather than persons. The sample used for analysis was reduced to individuals by counting the latest order imposed in 1993 on each person. The table shows the number of individual offences in the sample for cases matched with OI information. Offenders under 17 years old were also excluded so that valid comparisons could be made with the results reported by Lloyd et al (1994): probation was not available for such offenders in 1987. The right-hand column of Table 2.1 gives the number of offenders aged 17 years and over, which is the final dataset used in the analyses.

The table does not show probation with added requirements separately – only about 14 per cent of probation orders (455 offenders) in the sample had added requirements. The effect of disposal on reconviction is investigated in Chapter 5.

Though the sample is small for some of the areas, the numbers are large enough to detect any power that the most commonly collected social variables may have, when combined with criminal history variables, in predicting reconviction.

The definition of 'social' factor

The prediction methods currently in use are based on age, sex and criminal history. The other variables examined in this study are:

- 'dynamic' factors which affect offending, such as drug misuse or difficulties with accommodation or employment, which could be open to probation or other intervention;

---

2   From 1 October 1993 the term 'Probation Centre' replaced 'Day Centre'.

- 'dynamic' factors which may have a bearing on offending behaviour, but which may not be open to intervention, such as physical and mental health, marital status and responsibilities;

- 'static' factors, that is social characteristics that cannot be changed, such as ethnicity or having been a victim of abuse.

It is important to recognise that the information held on these factors is subjectively determined by a probation officer, even when the aspect of a problem under consideration is objective (for example, an offender either is or is not homeless). Such judgements are arrived at through a process of assessment which may or may not be systematic, but will almost certainly vary from officer to officer, and be recorded in a manner influenced by such things as local custom and procedure, available codings, design of forms, degree of conscientiousness and interviewing skill, and so on. They are not the product of objective or standardised assessment techniques, nor are they self-reports, which some other studies have used, for example Burnett (1994).

Significance testing

Throughout this report the statistical tests used are based on a significance level of 5 per cent, that is, any differences noted have a probability of only 5 per cent or less of occurring by chance.

Pseudo-reconvictions

Because the OI holds dates of reconviction rather than dates of reoffending, distortions in the data can occur. Firstly, a conviction may be recorded during the reconviction period, but relate to an offence that occurred before the current penalty was imposed. Secondly, an offender may commit an offence towards the end of the reconviction period but not be convicted of it until after the reconviction period. It was beyond the scope of this study to follow up in detail the effect of such 'pseudo-reconvictions'[3]. However, Lloyd et al (1994) showed that although the effect of pseudo-reconvictions was greater on the estimates of reconviction rates for community penalties than for prison, the effect was similar for each type of community disposal.

---

3   The term 'pseudo-reconviction' is generally applied to the first of these distortions, as it is more important to take it into account when making comparisons with reconviction rates for custody.

Table 2.1 Number of cases by disposal and area

	Orders made	Cases supplied by area	Matched with OI	Matched as percentage of cases supplied	Matched as percentage of orders made	Individuals, excluding juveniles
Cheshire						
Probation	715	741	656	89	92	587
CSO	853	866	744	86	87	656
Combination	153	155	142	92	93	128
All disposals	1,721	1,762	1,542	88	90	1,371
Dorset						
Probation	552	621	349	56	63	321
CSO	531	579	433	75	82	387
Combination	97	108	86	80	89	83
All disposals	1,180	1,308	868	66	74	791
Lincolnshire						
Probation	443	440	342	78	77	303
CSO	560	559	469	84	84	425
Combination	98	96	82	85	84	78
All disposals	1,101	1,095	893	82	81	806
Nottinghamshire						
Probation	1,038	1,069	903	84	87	844
CSO	1,010	1,004	860	86	85	799
Combination	163	165	142	86	87	125
All disposals	2,211	2,238	1,905	85	86	1,768
Oxfordshire & Bucks						
Probation	709	745	578	78	82	504
CSO	904	937	752	80	83	660
Combination	242	250	202	81	83	184
All disposals	1,855	1,932	1,532	79	83	1,348
NE London						
Probation	927	853	699	82	75	608
CSO	1,061	963	716	74	67	664
Combination	130	116	94	81	72	86
All disposals	2,118	1,932	1,509	78	71	1,358
All areas						
Probation	4,384	4,469	3,527	79	80	3,167
CSO	4,919	4,908	3,974	81	81	3,591
Combination	883	890	748	84	85	684
All disposals	10,186	10,267	8,249	80	81	7,442

3 The association of criminal history variables with reconviction

This chapter examines the relationship of criminal history variables (including age and sex) with reconviction rates, comparing the results of this study, where appropriate, with those reported by Lloyd et al (1994).

Area and disposal

Table 3.1 sets out two-year reconviction rates for each area by disposal type.

Table 3.1   Percentages reconvicted within two years of commencement by area and disposal

Probation area	Probation %	CSO %	Comb- ination %	n	Probation (OI) %	CSO (OI) %
Cheshire	64	48	60	1,371	67	53
Dorset	54	41	52	791	55	43
Lincolnshire	57	46	56	806	62	48
Nottinghamshire	49	44	54	1,768	51	46
Oxon & Bucks[4]	50	44	50	1,348	58/53	49/49
NE London	50	34	49	1,358	55	39
All six areas	53	43	53	7,442		
n	3,167	3,591	684	7,442		

The table shows that reconviction rates are lower for community service than for probation. There is also a variation across areas, with the rates for Cheshire being higher than average and those for Nottinghamshire (in particular probation) and NE London (in particular CSO) being lower than average. Whether the incidence of social variables can help to explain such regional differences is discussed in Chapter 6.

---

4   In 1993 Oxfordshire and Buckinghamshire were two separate services, hence the two figures for OI reconviction rates. The data for the study were supplied in 1997 by the amalgamated service and it was not possible to determine which cases came from which of the two original services.

The reconviction rates for probation orders in the sample are generally in line with those calculated on all cases from the Offenders Index (OI). These are given in the two right-hand columns of Table 3.1. For CSOs, however, there are significant differences for Cheshire, Oxfordshire & Buckinghamshire and NE London. There is no obvious explanation for this as there is no evidence that a systematic effect has caused certain types of case to be lost in the matching process.

Age and sex

In past studies reconviction has been found to be closely associated with both age and sex. Table 3.2 shows reconviction rates for the whole sample by age and sex.

Table 3.2   Percentages reconvicted by age and sex

Age	Male %	Female %	All %
17–20	64	46	63
21–24	55	44	54
25–29	48	34	46
30+	32	33	32
All ages	49	38	48
n	6,703	738	7,441

Note: Sex was missing for one case

The pattern shown here is very similar to that reported by Lloyd et al (1994) based on 1987 data[5], although the overall reconviction rate for this study is lower than for the previous one (48% compared with 55%). It should be noted, however, that the earlier sample included prisoners, and this may explain why the difference in reconviction rates is largest for males in the over-30 age group (32% compared with 42%). Figure 3.1 shows in more detail the relationship of reconviction with age and sex. Generally, reconviction goes down with increasing age and is lower for females than for males, especially below the age of 30. The line for females is more erratic than that for males because of the much smaller sample size.

Previous convictions

In line with the standard approach used for the probation service performance indicators, the measure of previous convictions adopted here is the number of previous court appearances at which the offender was found

---

5   Similar patterns for these variables and for some criminal history variables are shown for 1993 commencements in England and Wales, as reported in Kershaw (1997).

Figure 3.1 Reconviction by age and sex

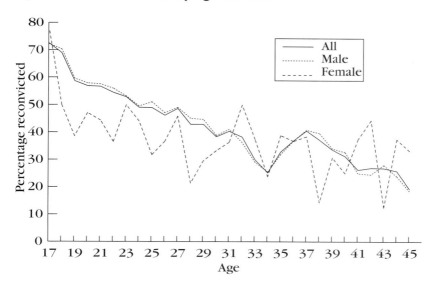

guilty, rather than counting every offence at each appearance. Figure 3.2 shows the relationship between reconviction and previous guilty appearances. The pattern is very similar to that reported by Lloyd et al (1994), with a steep rise in reconviction from none to about seven previous appearances, and a gentler rise with increasing appearances beyond seven.

Figure 3.2 Reconviction by previous guilty appearances

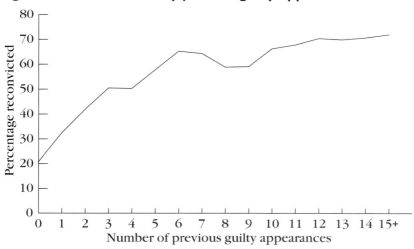

Females generally have lower numbers of previous guilty appearances than males (33% of females were first offenders compared with 13% of men) and so are likely to have lower reconviction rates[6]. However, for a given number of previous convictions the average rate of reconviction was similar for males and females. This was not found to be the case by Lloyd et al (1994), where reconviction was lower for females than males, even taking into account the number of previous convictions. Unfortunately it is not possible to say from this whether there has been a significant change in the pattern of female reconviction, as the present sample size for females is too small.

Previous custodial sentences

As in the previous research, reconviction was correlated to the number of both previous youth and adult custodial sentences, but more strongly to the former. For example, the reconviction rate for those with no experience of youth custody was 42 per cent, rising to 59 per cent for those with one previous youth custody. The corresponding figures for adult custody were 45 per cent and 55 per cent. The analysis in Chapter 5 examines whether this relationship holds even when the impact of previous convictions is taken into account (as previous custody and previous convictions are themselves related).

Rate of acquiring previous guilty appearances

Earlier research has shown that the rate of acquiring previous guilty appearances[7] is strongly related to reconviction. Figure 3.3 shows that reconviction generally increases with an increase in the rate. This mirrors the findings of Lloyd et al (1994).

Figure 3.3   Reconviction by rate of previous appearances

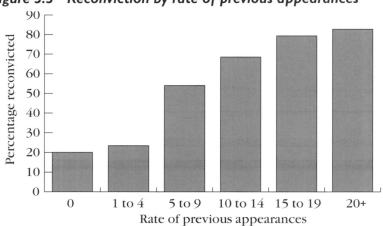

6   This finding is interesting in itself, and confirms the findings of Dowds and Hedderman (1997).
7   Lloyd et al defined this as: 10 x (number of appearances plus one) divided by (number of years since first appearance plus one), but with the rate set to zero for cases with no previous convictions. OGRS and KPI 1 use a different definition of appearance rate, and this has been used in the multivariate analyses (see Chapter 5).

Offence

Figure 3.4 shows reconviction rates for different principal offences as defined by the OI. The results are similar to those reported by Lloyd et al (1994), with low reconviction rates for sex offenders and high rates for burglary. There are some changes however, with a higher rate in this study for drug offences (46% compared with 35%), and a lower rate for criminal damage (45% compared with 60%).

The type of offence is correlated with other factors such as sex, age and previous convictions, and again the multivariate analysis discussed in Chapter 5 can help to disentangle these effects.

Figure 3.4 **Reconviction by current offence**

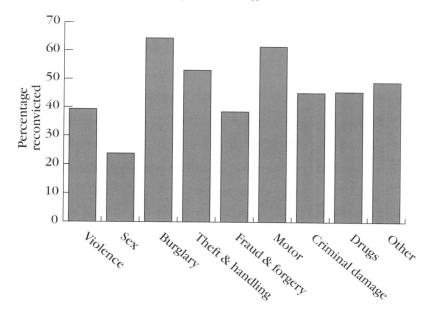

4 The social variables covered in the study

Table 4.1 shows the variables available for each area. More detail on the way in which the variables are coded is given in Appendix A. The table in the Appendix shows that while several factors are recorded by each area the coding systems are often very different. For example, a factor such as employment might be given a local factual code, perhaps recording such categories as 'permanent employment', 'temporary employment', 'casual', 'unemployed for under a year', 'unemployed for over a year', and so on. Alternatively, or in addition, a judgement might be made as to whether employment problems were affecting offending behaviour, and whether such effect was serious or moderate.

Table 4.1   The social variables available for each area

Variable	Cheshire	Dorset	Lincoln-shire	Notts	Oxon & Bucks	NE London
Accommodation	*	*	*	*	*	*
Employment	*	*	*	*	*	*
Alcohol	*	*	*	*	*	*
Drugs	*	*	*	*	*	*
Finance	*	*	*	*	*	*
Relationships	*	*	*	*	*	
Social Skills	*					
Literacy/learning problems	*	*		*		
Gambling				*		*
Mental health	*	*		*	*	*
Physical health	*	*		*		*
Ethnicity	*	*	*	*	*	*
Marital status/children		*				
Victim of physical abuse or violence		*		*		
Peer group			*			*
Other		*	*	*		*

The information available in the sample on social variables was recorded mainly at the start of the order (exceptions to this are noted in Appendix A). Dorset supplied information on terminations, but little can be deduced from it as the sample after matching was small. The best available information for both the start and the end of order was for employment and accommodation in the Oxfordshire & Buckinghamshire sample, although even with this there was a large proportion of unrecorded information at termination (about one-third). Assuming that there was no bias in the unrecorded cases, analysis indicated that there was a general tendency during the progress of a community penalty to move into more settled accommodation and into employment. Both these factors are associated with reduced reconviction. It is recognised that the data may be subject to the 'disclosure' effect noted by Aubrey and Hough (1997) – an apparent worsening of problems during supervision caused by more information coming to light or being revealed. However, the information we have for Oxfordshire & Buckinghamshire suggests that this is not the case.

Although ethnicity was recorded by each of the six areas, this information was too patchy to enable reliable conclusions to be drawn as to any link with reconviction. The five social variables on which usable information was available for all of the six study areas were: accommodation, employment, alcohol, drugs and finance. The separate relationships of these five variables with reconviction are considered in detail.

Accommodation

Cheshire – Reconviction rates were 56 per cent and 65 per cent for those with no problem and with a problem respectively. This difference is not significant, but the numbers involved are small. Only 4 per cent were recorded as having a problem with accommodation. The recording of other variables in Cheshire seems generally to be low.

Dorset – In about half of cases accommodation is not recorded; however reconviction is lower for owners (23%) and higher for those in lodgings or council rented accommodation (61% and 64% respectively).

Lincolnshire – 43 per cent of home-owners were reconvicted compared with 51 per cent for all cases (about half of all offenders were recorded as being home-owners – a higher than average percentage). 50 per cent of those with no problem were reconvicted compared with 70 per cent of those with an accommodation problem, although only 5 per cent were recorded as having a problem.

Nottinghamshire – 44 per cent of those with stable accommodation were reconvicted, compared with 62 per cent of those with unstable accommodation (16 % of the sample were in unstable accommodation).

Oxfordshire & Buckinghamshire – 42 per cent in settled accommodation were reconvicted compared with 52 per cent of those in unsettled (34% of sample were in unsettled accommodation).

NE London – The reconviction rate for those with accommodation problems was 46 per cent compared with 41 per cent for those without such problems; this difference, however, was not statistically significant. Those who were homeless had a high reconviction rate (61%), but the numbers were small – only 3 per cent were homeless.

It appears that accommodation is related to reconviction; where no difference was apparent the numbers involved were small. Some previous studies confirm this finding, but not very conclusively.

Employment

Cheshire – 52 per cent of those who had no problem with employment were reconvicted compared with 68 per cent of those with a problem (24% of offenders had a problem).

Dorset – As with accommodation, this was not recorded in about half of cases. It would therefore be misleading to say what proportion had a problem, but 58 per cent of those unemployed were reconvicted compared with 47 per cent for all cases.

Lincolnshire – 27 per cent of those permanently employed were reconvicted compared with 62 per cent of those unemployed for more than one year (36% of cases).

Nottinghamshire – 34 per cent in full-time employment were reconvicted compared with 57 per cent of those unemployed for more than one year (39% of cases).

Oxfordshire & Buckinghamshire – 29 per cent of those employed were reconvicted, while 52 per cent of those unemployed were reconvicted (66% of cases were unemployed).

NE London – 40 per cent of those unaffected by employment issues were reconvicted compared with 51 per cent of those so affected (25% of cases were affected).

Employment variables were, by themselves, significantly related to reconviction rates in each of the areas, and this result confirms the relationship found in other studies.

Alcohol

Cheshire – There was no significant relationship between alcohol problems and reconviction, but recording levels were low.

Dorset – 47 per cent of those without an alcohol problem were reconvicted, while 58 per cent with a problem were reconvicted (20% of cases had a problem).

Lincolnshire – No significant differences were found.

Nottinghamshire – 44 per cent of those not using substances[8] were reconvicted compared with 58 per cent of those using substances (18% of cases were users).

Oxfordshire & Buckinghamshire – No significant differences were found.

NE London – No significant differences were found.

Overall, the relationship between the use of alcohol and reconviction was clear in only one area. The evidence of previous studies is similarly unclear, but in a study of reconvictions in Kent, Oldfield (1996) reported a relationship.

Drugs

Cheshire – 52 per cent of those without a drug problem were reconvicted, while 79 per cent of those with a problem were reconvicted (16% of cases had a problem).

Dorset – 44 per cent of those without a drug problem were reconvicted, while 74 per cent of those with a problem were reconvicted (37% of cases were recorded as definitely not having a problem; 14% had or were likely to have a problem; the rest were unknown).

Lincolnshire – 50 per cent of those without a drug problem were reconvicted, while 69 per cent of those with a problem were reconvicted (however only 8% of cases were recorded as having a problem).

Nottinghamshire – see *'Alcohol'* above.

Oxfordshire & Buckinghamshire – 44 per cent of those without a drug problem were reconvicted, while 64 per cent of those with a problem were reconvicted (14% of cases had a problem).

---

8   There was a technical problem with the Nottinghamshire data which made it impossible to separate the different types of substance misuse, ie drugs, alcohol and other substances.

NE London – 40 per cent of those whose offending was unaffected by drug use were reconvicted compared with 72 per cent of those whose offending was affected. The difference is very significant even though only 7 per cent were affected by drug use.

Drug use was highly related to reconviction in all areas. The apparent variations in the occurrence of drug problems between areas are probably due to differences in definition and recording. Burnett (1994) found that offenders with drug problems were themselves more likely to predict that they would reoffend.

Financial problems

Cheshire – 53 per cent of those without financial problems were reconvicted compared with 67 per cent of those with problems. Recording was low.

Dorset – In this area the size of debt was coded but was not recorded in nearly half of cases. There is mixed evidence about the relationship with reconviction according to the size of debt.

Lincolnshire – There was only a weak relationship between debt problems and reconviction, even though 25 per cent of cases had a problem.

Nottinghamshire – 44 per cent of those with no debt were reconvicted, while 50 per cent with debt were reconvicted. 34 per cent of those not on benefit were reconvicted compared with 52 per cent of those on benefit (73% of offenders were on benefit).

Oxfordshire & Buckinghamshire – 44 per cent with no financial problems were reconvicted, while 52 per cent with a problem were reconvicted (38% of cases had a problem).

NE London – There was no significant difference in reconviction rates between those whose offending was or was not affected by lack of money (24% of cases were affected).

Overall, the evidence on the connection between financial circumstances and reconviction is fairly weak, but, again, Oldfield (1996) found a relationship.

Other social variables

Some of the variables that may be associated with reconviction but which are not available for each of the areas are discussed here. In previous studies **marital status** has been found to be significant. It was recorded in about half of cases in Dorset. The reconviction rates for single offenders and those with partners were virtually identical. Similarly, there was no evidence from the Dorset data that having dependent children is correlated with reconviction.

Physical and mental health variables did not appear to be correlated with reconviction in any of the areas recording them, nor did any of the previous studies examined report an association. **Peer group** pressure and problems with **relationships** were significantly associated with reconviction (this was confirmed by some previous studies). Being a past **victim of violence**, recorded only in Nottinghamshire, was also correlated with reconviction. In the two areas where **literacy problems** were recorded, offenders with such problems were more likely to be reconvicted; however, the numbers involved were too small to establish statistical significance. In a third area **learning problems** were significantly related to reconviction – 46 per cent of those without learning difficulties were reconvicted compared with 62 per cent of those with such difficulties.

The initial analyses did not find evidence of a direct relationship between some social variables, for example health and marital status, and reconviction. However, all the available valid variables were included in the separate multivariate analyses for areas in case they had any predictive power in conjunction with other variables.

The variation of reconviction with different combinations of social factors

The analysis described above shows that there are links, whether strong or weak, between each of the five common social variables and reconviction. To identify whether an accumulation of problems increases the likelihood of reconviction, Table 4.2 sets out the relationship between the numbers of social factors (or 'problems') recorded for each offender and average reconviction rates.

Table 4.2   Numbers of problems and reconviction

Number of problems recorded	Percentage reconvicted	n
0	43.7	1,947
1	46.0	1,401
2	49.0	1,146
3	56.1	757
4	64.4	362
5	77.0	61
All cases	48.6	5,674

Excludes Nottinghamshire, for which drug and alcohol problems could not be counted separately.

Table 4.2 shows clearly that the reconviction rate rises with increased numbers of problems. It is possible that particular types of problem occurring together could be linked with increased reconviction rates. This was tested by examining the average reconviction rates for each possible combination of the five main social variables. The clearest pattern that emerged was the relationship between reconviction and drugs problems. Drugs featured in each of the 11 combinations with the highest reconviction rates, and in none of the ten combinations with the lowest rates. The pattern for employment problems was to some extent similar, but was not as marked. Accommodation and alcohol (especially the latter) were the problems most likely to occur in combinations with lower reconviction rates, but they also figured in groups with high rates.

In order to take account of the relationship between reconviction and multiple problems, the combinations of the five main social factors have been included in the logistic regression analyses described in the next chapter.

Relationships between criminal history and social variables

The relationships between criminal history variables and the social variables have been examined, as in the statistical analysis the effects of social factors tend to be confounded by any correlation between them and the criminal history variables. Firstly, simple binary relationships were studied, comparing each criminal history variable (current age, sex, offence, previous guilty appearances and previous custody) with each of the five main social variables. The following relationships were found.

- Accommodation problems generally decrease with age.

- Employment problems decrease with age, increase with numbers of previous appearances, and are higher for some offences (in particular burglary, theft of or from motor cars and criminal damage).

- Financial problems are higher for females, and for some offences (fraud & forgery, theft & handling, motor offences and burglary).

- Problems with alcohol and drugs were both related to each of the criminal history variables examined. Alcohol problems are more frequent with increasing age, for males, for violent offences and criminal damage and for increasing previous guilty appearances and custody. Drug problems decrease with age, are more frequent for females, are (unsurprisingly) associated with drug offences, and increase with increasing previous appearances and custody.

Secondly, the more complex relationships of social variables with pairs of criminal history variables were examined graphically. The mean of each social variable for different values of one criminal history was plotted against another criminal history variable. This made it possible to see if there were instances where offenders with certain combinations of different criminal history variables were more likely to have particular social problems. The following relationships were apparent.

- Accommodation problems were higher for offenders under 21 and remained fairly constant with increasing guilty appearances. For older offenders there were fewer accommodation problems but they increased slightly with increasing guilty appearances (Figure 4.1).

Figure 4.1 Percentage with accommodation problems by number of previous guilty appearances and age

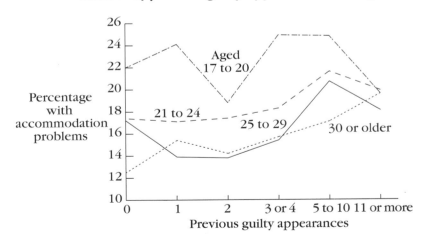

- For males, employment problems decreased with increasing age. For those under 21 and those aged 30 or over employment problems were similar for females and males. However, for females in their twenties employment problems were lower. It could perhaps be speculated that women in their twenties are more likely to be caring for children and a home so lack of employment would not be considered as a problem (Figure 4.2).

Figure 4.2   Percentage with employment problems by age and sex

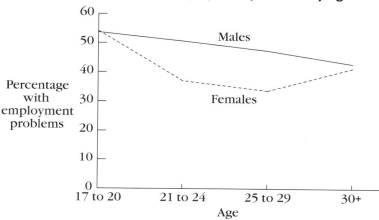

- Financial problems are especially high for offenders aged under 21 with many previous guilty appearances or with previous custody, and also for offenders in their early twenties convicted of fraud & forgery. Financial problems were also high for those in their late twenties convicted of theft of or from motor vehicles; however, the sample for these was small (Figures 4.3 and 4.4).

Figure 4.3   Percentage with financial problems by previous guilty appearances and age

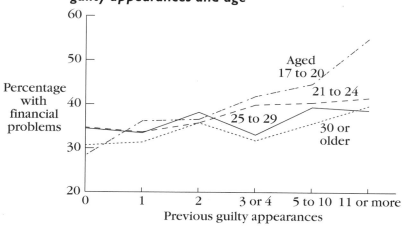

Figure 4.4   Percentage with financial problems by age and offence

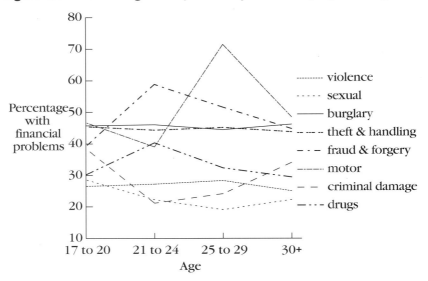

- For females, financial problems are not related to previous guilty appearances; for males, financial problems are less frequent, but increase slightly with increasing numbers of previous appearances (Figure 4.5).

Figure 4.5   Percentage with financial problems by previous guilty appearances and sex

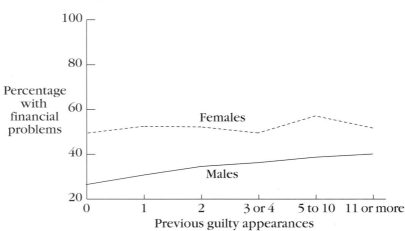

- Alcohol problems are less frequent for females than for males, and also increase less with increasing age (Figure 4.6).

Figure 4.6 Percentage with alcohol problems by age and sex

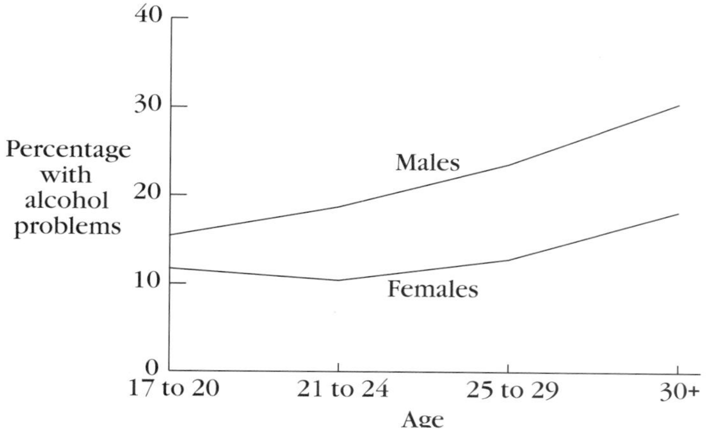

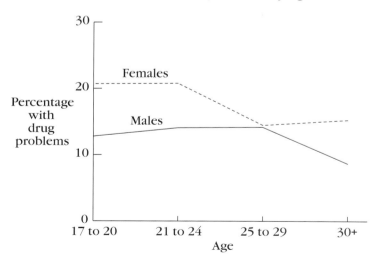

- While for both males and females drugs problems decrease with age, and generally females are more likely to have drugs problems than males, the pattern of the reduction is such that for those in their late twenties similar proportions of males and females have problems (Figure 4.7).

Figure 4.7 Percentage with drug problems by age and sex

The relationships that have been found between the criminal history and social variables can help to inform the discussion of the logistic regressions in the next chapter.

Summary of this chapter

This chapter has shown that:

- the recording of social variables is inconsistent;

- where systems exist to record social variables they are often not used fully;

- the categories used in the coding systems do not always recognise the need to record both factual and judgmental information separately;

- nevertheless there are clear links between social factors and reconviction.

The deficiencies in the information available on social variables do not allow its full potential to be realised in terms of useful and sensible conclusions. It also helps to explain why previous studies have yielded mixed results, and has implications for practitioners in the consistent assessment of offenders across probation services.

5 The use of social variables to improve prediction

The relationship between reconviction and the factors associated with it has been tested using the statistical technique of logistic regression. This method helps to show whether a relationship between two factors still holds when other factors are taken into account. For example, does the fact that older offenders are less likely to be reconvicted hold true regardless of how many previous convictions they have? In other words, is being older or being an infrequent offender the 'determining' factor? Logistic regression helps to disentangle such effects caused by relationships between the variables. It uses variables to produce an equation that predicts the probability of a particular outcome, in this instance reconviction. For each offender, the probability can be turned into a prediction: for probabilities over 0.5, reconviction is predicted (in other words, it is more than 50% likely that the offender will be reconvicted). One of the main aims of this study is to determine whether the social variables can add predictive power to the mainly criminal history variables already used for prediction. The approach taken has therefore been to compare analyses that exclude social variables with analyses that include them, examining what improvement, if any, the factors add to the prediction.

The criminal history variables (including age and sex) taken into consideration in the analyses are:

- Age at current sentence
- Sex
- Current offence
- Number of previous court appearances at which found guilty
- Number of previous youth imprisonments
- Rate of acquiring previous guilty appearances[9]

These variables are the main ones found to be significant in predicting reconviction by Lloyd et al (1994).

Two main sets of analyses were performed:

- the first covered each probation area separately, looking at all the social variables available for each area;

---

9   Calculated as 75 x $\sqrt{((\text{previous guilty appearances} + 1)/(\text{years between first and current conviction} + 5))}$. This is used in OGRS.

- the second used the data for all areas, including only those social variables (as described in Chapter 4) for which some measure was available in every area.

For each of the five 'common' social variables a composite variable was formed which indicated whether a particular factor was regarded as a problem and might affect offending behaviour. These composite variables are not ideal because of the differences in coding between areas, exacerbated by low levels of recording of some variables. However, the analyses using the composite variables formed a useful supplement to the analyses by area, confirming the results with a larger sample.

Interactions between the predictor variables

A predictor variable may have a direct relationship by itself with the predicted variable (in this instance reconviction), but may also have a relationship in combination with another variable or variables. For example, being under 21 *and* having previously been in custody may increase the chance of reconviction much more than the effect of the two variables separately. This increased effect of two or more variables together is known as an interaction.

Interactions between predictor variables were examined using a technique in which the sample was repeatedly divided and subdivided according to the values of that predictor variable which had the greatest influence on the reconviction rate. The results of this method are shown in the tree diagram beginning at Chart A. The top box shows the whole sample, 7,441 cases[10] with an average reconviction rate of 48.2 per cent. The first division was made according to the number of previous guilty appearances: those with three or more have an average rate of 60.8 per cent, while those with under three have a rate of only 30.7 per cent. Each of these two samples was further subdivided as shown in Charts B and C. The process was continued until the sample in a box became small (under 100 was chosen in this instance) or if no variable could be found giving rise to two subgroups with significantly different reconviction rates.

It is notable that all the first subdivisions of the sample were based on age and numbers of previous guilty appearances, even though other variables were considered (previous youth and adult custody, sex, offence and social variables). At the end of some branches divisions were made on the basis of social variables, but not on the basis of criminal history variables other than age and number of previous guilty appearances. This is interesting in that it implies, even when age and previous appearances are taken into account,

---

10   One of the factors considered (sex) was not available for one case.

firstly that social variables are still linked with differences in reconviction rates, and secondly that this association is stronger than that of other criminal history factors.

Chart A   *Tree diagram of the interaction of factors affecting reconviction*

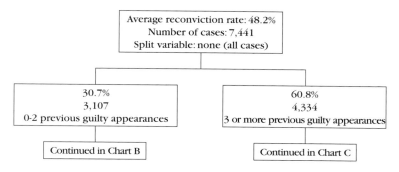

The repeated division of the sample (based on combinations of predictor factors) splits the whole sample into a number of subgroups with differing average reconviction rates. The groups are listed in Table C.1 in Appendix C. At one end of the range is Group 1 which is made up of offenders aged 28 or more with no or one previous guilty appearance and no financial problems; these have an average reconviction rate of under 9 per cent. At the other end is Group 23 whose members are aged 17 to 23 and have 12 or more previous guilty appearances; these have an average reconviction rate of 93 per cent.

Each offender's group membership can be used in the logistic regression analyses to take into account interactions between the predictor variables. The groups that were not based on a division by a social factor were entered into the first set of analyses along with the criminal history variables. In order to include all available information on interactions, the 'parents' of the final groups involving social factors were entered also; these are shown as Groups A, B, C, and D in Table C.1. For example, Group A, which can be divided according to financial problems to form Groups 1 and 2, is not itself based on a division by a social factor. The remaining groups (those based on division by social factor) were entered into the second set of analyses, along with the social variables and their interactions.

Chart B   Tree diagram of the interaction of factors affecting reconviction – continued from Chart A

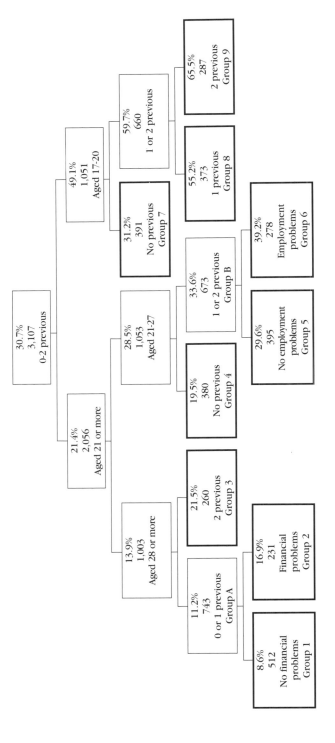

Note: 'previous' signifies 'previous guilty appearances'.

Chart C   Tree diagram of the interaction of factors affecting reconviction – continued from Chart A

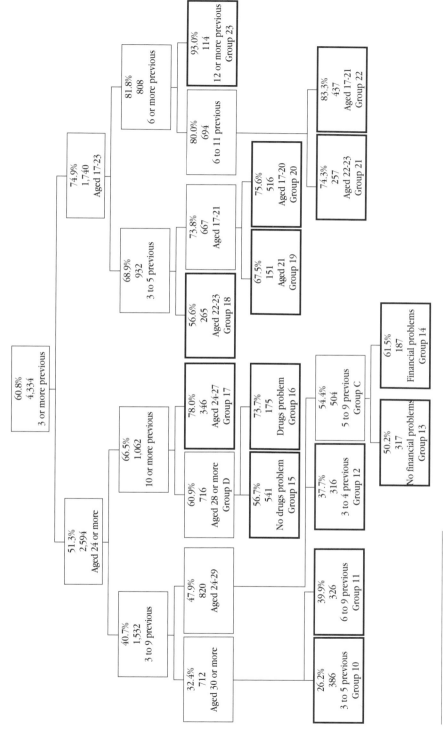

Note: 'previous' signifies 'previous guilty appearances'.

The multivariate analyses

The results of the analyses

Table 5.1 gives the results of the logistic regression analysis for all six areas. Analyses were made also for each area separately. (Tables B.1 and B.2 in Appendix B give further details of the results of the regression models with and without the addition of social variables.) The criminal history variable that was found to be of greatest significance for each area and for the model for all six areas together was the rate of acquiring previous guilty appearances. Less significant, but chosen for most areas, was current age; age also appeared for each area in terms of the interaction groups. Table 5.1 shows which variables had a negative coefficient in the model; this indicates an inverse relationship with reconviction. Thus the coefficient for current age is negative, meaning that reconviction generally becomes less likely as age increases.

Table 5.1 Results of logistic regressions for all six areas together

Significant variables (in descending order of significance)	Sign
Increasing rate of guilty appearances	+
Offence: burglary	+
theft & handling	+
Group 4 (aged 21–27, no previous)	–
Increasing age	–
Group B (aged 21–27, 1–2 previous)	–
Drugs	**+**
Alcohol*drugs	**–**
Group 7 (aged 17–20, no previous)	–
Increasing previous occurrences of adult custody	+
Group 12 (aged 24–29, 3–4 previous)	–
Accommodation*alcohol*drugs*employment	**+**
Group A (aged 28+, 0–1 previous)	–
Increasing numbers of previous guilty appearances	–
Group C (aged 24–29, 5–9 previous)	–
Group 1 (aged 28+, 0–1 previous, no financial problems)	**+**
Group 23 (aged 17–23, 12+ previous)	+
Group 14 (aged 24–29, 5–9 previous, financial problems)	**+**
Group 22 (aged 17–21, 6–11 previous)	+
Group 16 (aged 28+, 10+ previous, drugs problem)	**+**
Group 3 (aged 28+, 2 previous)	–

Notes: 'Previous' signifies 'previous guilty appearances'.
        Factors involving social problems are shown in bold type.

Previous adult custody was significant in the model for all six areas; it was associated with increased likelihood of reconviction. Previous youth custody was not significant once other variables had been taken into account. Consistent with the previous research, the sex of the offender was not significantly associated with reconviction once other variables were entered into the model. Offence type was significant for the analysis covering all six areas. The significant offence types were burglary and theft & handling, both of whose coefficients were positive, indicating that offenders with these offences were more likely to be reconvicted. These results tally with those of previous research.

The social variable that features most commonly in the analyses is problems with drugs, either as an effect in itself or in interaction with other variables. It was significant for each of the five areas where a distinction between drug and alcohol misuse was available. Generally, the relationship is clear – drug misusers were more likely to be reconvicted. The analysis cannot reveal the mechanism whereby drug misuse (or indeed any of the other factors) can lead to a higher risk of reconviction, but its interaction with employment problems in three areas is consistent with the possibility that drug misusers commit crime to finance the habit. It is notable that despite the correlation of drug problems with age, this was still a significant factor.

As well as appearing in interactions with drug problems, employment problems appeared with alcohol and financial problems, and was significant for offenders aged 21 to 27 with one or two previous guilty appearances.

In addition to drug misuse and employment problems, each of the other three variables that were available in some form in all six areas features in the final models. It was seen earlier when looking at alcohol problems that the evidence across the six areas did not present a clear picture. The more detailed analysis shows that alcohol misuse plays a part in reconviction, but not in a straightforward way. It was significant for only one area (in an interaction with employment and financial problems) and for all six areas together. However, in the overall model alcohol featured in two different interactions, one positively and one negatively related to reconviction. Further research is needed to clarify the relationship between alcohol misuse and reconviction.

Accommodation problems featured only for Nottinghamshire and the overall model, being associated with increased reconviction. Financial problems were included in two area models, standing alone and in interaction with alcohol misuse and employment problems. It was associated with an increased chance of reconviction.

The effect of multiple social problems appeared in the analysis of all areas as an interaction between accommodation, alcohol, drugs and employment problems. This means that offenders with all four of these problems have a significantly higher chance of being reconvicted. The model for Dorset included the interaction of three factors: alcohol, employment and financial problems.

None of the other social variables (those not available in all six areas) was significant once other factors had been included.

Interpretation of the results of the analyses should be approached carefully. Because some factors are similar in predictive power, in selecting the interaction groups even slight variations in the data could result in different splits and so lead to different final groups. It is important, therefore, in looking at the results of the analyses not to put too much emphasis on the interpretation in detail of the interaction effects. The aim of the analysis has been to extract the maximum information from the current data based on criminal history variables, and then to see whether social variables can add further to the prediction of reconviction. The detail of the results, however, should not be applied to other data sets: further work is required using more consistent and more accurately recorded social factors to construct a more reliable and generalisable model.

As it is difficult to interpret the interaction effects, analyses were made in which only the straight social variables were added to the models based on criminal history variables. Taking all areas together, the significant social factors were substance misuse (alcohol and/or drugs) and employment problems. For the five areas for which drug and alcohol misuse could be distinguished drug misuse was the significant social factor. Looking at areas separately, drug misuse was significant for four of the five areas for which this variable was available. Employment and financial problems were each significant for two areas, and accommodation problems were significant for one area. For Lincolnshire only, when interactions were not included, none of the five main social factors was significant; the *number* of social problems, however, was significant.

Measuring the contribution that social factors make in prediction

In looking at the results of the logistic regression analyses it is necessary to *measure* the effect of adding social variables. The very fact that a variable is chosen to be entered into the model means that its effect is statistically significant – but what does this mean in terms of the practical uses to which prediction is put? Two of the main uses of reconviction prediction are:

- to assess the probability of reconviction of an individual (for example OGRS); and

- to predict average reconviction rates in order to compare the effects of disposal (for example performance indicators).

There are several ways of indicating the predictive power of a model. One commonly used measure is the number of cases predicted correctly. For each offender a model gives the predicted probability (on a scale from 0 to 1) of the risk of being reconvicted. If this probability is below 0.5 the prediction is that the offender will not be reconvicted; if it is above 0.5 it is predicted that the offender will be reconvicted. These predictions can be compared with the actual reconviction data to give the percentage correctly predicted. The model can be wrong in two ways. It can predict that someone is likely to be reconvicted, but they are not (a 'false positive'); or that someone is unlikely to be reconvicted but they are (a 'false negative').

Both forms of inaccuracy may have undesirable consequences, generating civil liberties concern in the case of false positives and endangering the public in the case of false negatives. The following discussion focuses on false negatives for simplicity, but that should not be taken to imply that false positives are seen as unimportant.

Methods that involve contrasting the actual and predicted reconviction rates and checking for false negatives have a weakness – they do not take account of the level of risk predicted for each offender, but only whether the predicted risk is above or below 0.5. This means that only those offenders whose predicted risk crosses the 0.5 line when social variables are added are included in the measures. A third, more sophisticated, method that includes all cases is to examine the change in the predicted probability case by case, looking at both the size of a change and its direction, that is, whether the predicted risk is improved or worsened. To do this a 'measure of improvement' has been devised, calculated as the ratio of the total change in risk for cases with an improvement to the change in risk for all cases. If there were no overall improvement but merely a random change in prediction this measure (expressed as a percentage) would be 50 per cent. This value forms a baseline for the measure, with values greater than 50 per cent indicating an overall improvement in prediction.

Table 5.2   Results of logistic regressions for each area separately, and for all six areas together: measures of the effect of including social variables

Area	Criminal history variables alone		Criminal history plus social variables		Improvement measure
	Percentage predicted correctly	Percentage of false negatives	Percentage predicted correctly	Percentage of false negatives	
Cheshire	74.9	11.4	75.0	11.2	54.3
Dorset	70.5	16.1	70.2	16.3	61.0
Lincolnshire	69.2	15.0	69.7	15.0	59.3
Nottinghamshire	72.2	15.3	72.4	15.1	56.7
Oxon & Bucks	68.8	15.9	71.4	15.1	60.6
NE London	71.2	17.9	72.8	16.3	63.1
All six areas	71.6	13.6	72.1	13.4	57.1

Table 5.2 shows that adding social variables to the criminal history variables for each separate area model slightly increases the percentage of cases predicted correctly for five areas, and very slightly decreases it in the sixth (Dorset). For five of the six areas the number of 'false negatives' is reduced, the exception again being Dorset. For Dorset (as for each of the other areas) the improvement measure is over 50 per cent. This indicates that, averaged over each case, there is an improvement in prediction, even though there is a worsening in terms of the percentage predicted correctly (that is a higher number of cases cross the 0.5 boundary in the wrong direction, rather than the right).

Adding social variables to the model for all six areas slightly increases the number predicted correctly, and also reduces the number of 'false negatives', that is those who are predicted as unlikely to be reconvicted, but who are reconvicted.

How well do the logistic regression models fit the data?

As pointed out above, the number of cases predicted correctly is a crude measure of how well the models fit the data. In the earlier research by Lloyd et al (1994) the distribution of the predicted risk scores was compared with actual reconvictions. The distribution for the present model is shown in Table 5.3.

Table 5.3   Proportion actually reconvicted by predicted risk of reconviction

a.   Model with criminal history variables only

	Predicted risk of reconviction (per cent)									
	0 to 10	>10 to 20	>20 to 30	>30 to 40	>40 to 50	>50 to 60	>60 to 70	>70 to 80	>80 to 90	>90 to 100
Actual percentage reconvicted	6	16	24	33	48	57	66	75	83	93
n	356	732	1,052	923	926	809	866	894	656	228

b.   Model with criminal history and social variables

	Predicted risk of reconviction (per cent)									
	0 to 10	>10 to 20	>20 to 30	>30 to 40	>40 to 50	>50 to 60	>60 to 70	>70 to 80	>80 to 90	>90 to 100
Actual percentage reconvicted	7	15	24	33	47	60	64	75	84	92
n	412	764	1,025	924	855	782	811	915	667	287

The table shows that the actual proportion reconvicted in each prediction category falls within the appropriate band, and often near the mid-point. This indicates a good fit. The distribution for the model with social variables gives a similar picture.

In summary, the results indicate that social variables are significantly related to reconviction but that their effect in improving prediction is only very slight. However, inconsistencies of coding across probation areas meant that some of the variations in the social variables were apparent rather than real. It is likely that this weakened the predictive effect of the social variables.

The effect of social factors on predicting reconviction early in criminal careers

It is possible that social factors could be more influential for offenders who have no previous court appearances, or just a few. To examine this proposition, separate regression analyses were performed for offenders with less than three previous guilty appearances, and for the remaining offenders with three or more. (This particular division is that suggested by the 'tree diagram' analysis of interactions.) The aim was to see whether adding social variables to the model improved the prediction of reconviction more for the former model than for the latter.

There is some evidence (see Table 5.4) that social factors are more significant in predicting reconviction for those with under three previous guilty appearances. Each of the five social factors appeared either singly or in an interaction in the model for those with under three appearances, whereas employment problems did not feature for the sample including only those with three or more previous appearances. Criminal history featured more heavily for the latter sample, including (unlike the other model) adult imprisonment and type of offence. The measure of improvement is also greater for less than three appearances than for three or more. This suggests that a knowledge of social factors is especially important for cases with little criminal history, and that practitioners need timely and accurate social information on which to base an assessment of risk.

The effect of sentence

Characteristics of the disposal groups

Table 3.1 in Chapter 3 showed that there are considerable differences in reconviction rates between different disposal groups. Is it possible to say how far these differences are due to the characteristics of the offenders given different community sentences, and how much could be attributed to the effects of the disposal itself?

The characteristics of the disposal groups have been examined in terms of factors that have been seen to be related to reconviction. About 18 per cent of those given probation without conditions were female, compared with an average of less than 6 per cent of the other disposals. As sex is associated with reconviction, and the explanatory variables often differ by sex (for example, women generally have fewer previous guilty appearances) for simplicity of interpretation Table 5.5 includes males only.

The table summarises the criminal history and social characteristics for each of the four disposal groups, showing for comparison the reconviction rates for each disposal. The reconviction rate is higher than average for those sentenced to probation with added requirements, and lower for those on community service.

The proportions in the high risk age group do not differ significantly. Lloyd et al (1994) found that of those with straight probation a lower proportion was in this age group. This may reflect a move over recent years towards probation dealing with more offenders convicted of serious offences.

Table 5.4   Results of logistic regressions on samples split by number of previous guilty appearances

	Sample with 0 to 2 previous guilty appearances		Sample with 3 or more previous guilty appearances	
Significant variables (in order of significance)	Increasing rate of guilty appearances Group 8 (aged 17–20, 1 previous) **Drugs*finance** **Alcohol*drugs*finance** (−) Increasing age (−) Group 9 (aged 17–20, 2 previous) **Accommodation*alcohol*drugs** **Group 1 (aged 28+, 0 or 1 previous, no financial problems)** (−) **Employment problems** Previous guilty appearances Group 7 (aged 17–20, no previous)		Increasing rate of guilty appearances Type of offence (burglary, theft & handling) Increasing age (−) Group 12 (aged 24–29, 3–4 previous) (−) Adult imprisonment **Drugs** **Alcohol*drugs** (−) Group C (aged 24–29, 5–9 previous) (−) Previous guilty appearances (−) Group 18 (aged 22–23, 3–5 previous) (−) **Accommodation*drugs** Group 23 (aged 17–23, 12+ previous) Group 10 (aged 30+, 3–5 previous) (−) **Alcohol*finances** Female	
Percentage predicted correctly (without and with social factors)	73.8	74.1	70.5	70.9
Percentage of false negatives (without and with social factors)	18.7	18.1	9.8	10.0
Measure of improvement from addition of social factors[11]	60.7		56.5	

11   The method of calculating this measure is described earlier in this chapter.

39

Table 5.5   A comparison of characteristics by disposal – percentages with given risk characteristics (males only)

Variable	Straight Probation	Probation with requirements	Community Service Order	Combin- ation Order
Aged 17–20	26	25	26	28
6+ previous guilty appearances	44	49	31	40
Previous youth imprisonment	36	37	25	37
Previous appearance rate of 10+[12]	43	48	31	39
High risk offences[13]	45	41	40	39
Unemployed	57	56	41	56
Alcohol/drugs problems	47	52	21	40
Accommodation problems	27	26	12	24
Financial problems	44	25	30	38
Actual two-year reconviction rate	55	59	44	54
n	2,240	422	3,400	641

Probation with requirements shows the highest rate of previous court appearances resulting in conviction, followed by straight probation and combination orders. A lower percentage of those with community service orders than those with other disposals had six or more previous appearances. The proportion that had served youth custody was also low for community service, but there was less difference between the disposals in the prevalence of high risk current offences. The overall picture is of larger proportions of high risk characteristics for those given probation with requirements, followed by straight probation, combination orders and community service orders. It appears, therefore, that sentencers use probation for most serious offenders and community service for the less serious. This pattern is reflected in the relative reconviction rates for these four disposals. It confirms the findings reported by Lloyd et al (1994), although the relationship is not so pronounced.

Table 5.5 also includes the key social factors recorded by all six areas. Each of the variables shows large differences between some of the disposals. Problems with alcohol and drugs are particularly high for added requirements. This is not simply because the added requirements were for the treatment of substance misuse as only 9 per cent of added requirements

12   The appearance rate used by Lloyd et al (1994) is used here for purposes of comparison.
13   High risk offences were defined by Lloyd et al (1994) in HORS 136 as burglary, theft, criminal damage and motor offences. This is used for comparison here. A new definition might include drug offences, but it has been found in this study that doing so does not reveal any further link between offence and reconviction rate.

were specifically for drug/alcohol treatment. Problems were least common for community service – accommodation problems were also low and fewer offenders were unemployed than in the other disposal groups. Proportions with financial problems were high for those on straight probation, but low for those with added requirements and those on community service. This result for those with added requirements is perhaps surprising, being the only instance of a characteristic that appears not to tally with the probability of reconviction. However, it could be due to the fact that the area recording the highest levels of financial problems also happens to have the lowest proportion of cases with added requirements; and, whilst the result is statistically significant, the sample involved is small.

The results for females (not given in detail as the sample size is small) confirm that at one end of the spectrum those with added requirements tend to exhibit high risk characteristics, while at the other end those on community service have lower proportions of the risk factors. This is consistent with the pattern of reconviction across disposal groups. In other words it would seem that differences in the reconviction rates between disposals are consistent with the characteristics of those given different sentences.

Factors affecting the choice of disposal

The technique that was used to look at the interaction of factors affecting reconviction was used again to examine what factors affect the choice of disposal. In this case the divisions of the sample were based on examining variations in the percentage given a community service order as opposed to probation or combination orders. (The numbers given probation with requirements or combination orders were too small for this type of analysis to be effective.) The tree diagram is shown in Chart D and the subgroups resulting from the analysis are given in Table C.2 in Appendix C. The first divisions in the 'tree' are based on substance misuse and sex, and social variables mostly figure higher in the tree than criminal history variables. Females are less likely than males to be given a community service order, in particular those with substance misuse or financial problems. The three groups most likely to be given a community service order are all composed of males with no social problems. Those with previous guilty appearances are generally less likely to be put on community service, but even those with 10 or more such appearances, if they are also male and have no social problems, have a higher than average probability of being given a community service order.

Chart D   Interaction of the factors affecting Community Service as the choice of disposal

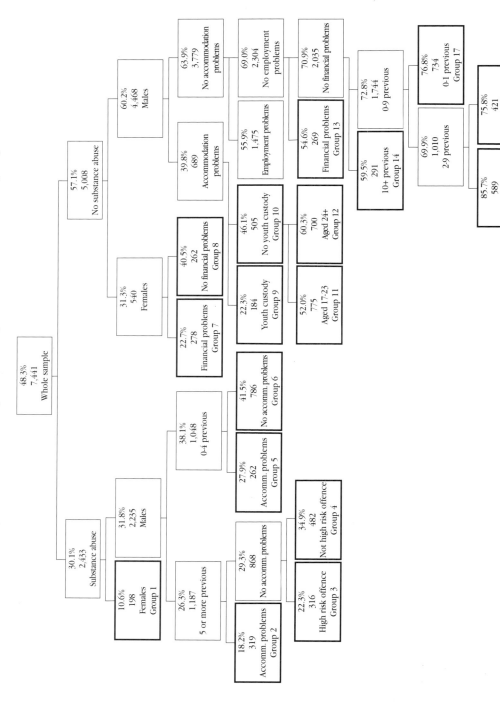

This analysis shows that while social factors may have limited scope in adding to the prediction of reconviction, they are potentially very important in studies of the choice of disposal or 'targeting'. There are undoubtedly sound reasons for the differences in offenders' characteristics for different sentences; however the results prompt such policy questions as: 'Should there be better community service provision for women?' and 'Should sentencers be encouraged to consider community service more seriously for offenders with social problems?'.

Disposal and reconviction

The analyses summarised in Tables 5.1, B.1 and B.2 do not include disposal type; the predicted reconviction rates from these models are therefore based solely on the criminal history and social variables. Table 5.6 gives (for males and females together) the actual reconviction rates for each disposal, first based on criminal history variables only, and secondly including the significant social variables.

Each of the predicted rates for the models without social factors differs significantly from the corresponding actual rates. Including social variables improves the predicted rates of reconviction for straight probation and community service, although the predicted rate for community service still differs significantly from the actual rate. The addition of social variables has no apparent effect on the prediction for probation with requirements or combination orders.

Table 5.6　Actual and predicted reconviction rates by disposal

	Straight Probation	Probation with requirements	Community Service	Combination Order	All disposals
Actual percentage reconvicted	52.7	57.6	42.7	53.4	48.2
Predicted percentage reconvicted (criminal history variables only)	51.3*	54.7*	44.6*	50.9*	48.2
Predicted percentage reconvicted (criminal history + social variables)	52.4	55.2	43.7*	51.2*	48.2
n	2,712	455	3,591	684	7,442

* Significantly different from actual rate.

Whether disposal group has any predictive power in addition to the other variables can be tested by adding it as another factor in the logistic regression analyses. The addition of type of disposal to the models (see Table 5.7) added only marginally or not at all to their predictive power. For NE London and for all areas taken together the low predicted reconviction rate for community service was not fully explained by the criminal history and social variables. In other words, the disposal itself slightly improved the prediction model. For NE London, community service is less significant than drugs problems and the criminal history variables, but more significant than any of the interactions. In the analysis for all areas, community service is a more significant factor than four interaction groups, including interactions with drugs and financial problems. Although disposal is a weak predictor compared with criminal history factors, the results suggest (even taking into account other variables) that what happens during a sentence may have a positive effect on future offending behaviour.

Table 5.7   The effect of disposal on the prediction of reconviction rates

Area	Criminal history and social variables		Criminal history, social variables and disposal			
	Percentage predicted correctly	Percentage of false negatives	Percentage predicted correctly	Percentage of false negatives	Improvement measure	Significant disposal group
Cheshire	75.0	11.2	75.0	11.2	-	None
Dorset	70.2	16.3	70.2	16.3	-	None
Lincolnshire	69.7	15.0	69.7	15.0	-	None
Nottinghamshire	72.4	15.1	72.4	15.1	-	None
Oxon & Bucks	71.4	15.1	71.4	15.1	-	None
NE London	72.8	16.3	72.9	16.0	53.9	Community service
All six areas	72.1	13.4	72.0	13.6	51.5	Community service

6 Differences in reconviction rates between areas

As Table 3.1 showed, there are considerable differences in the raw reconviction rates for each type of disposal between the six areas in the study. This chapter examines whether the differences between areas can be explained by criminal history, social factors or disposal type.

The incidence of risk characteristics of male offenders for the two disposal groups of straight probation and community service were compared. (The sample was too small to give valid results for probation with requirements and combination orders, or for female offenders.) Social variables were included but the differences between areas in their recording and coding meant that comparisons had to be made with great care.

For straight probation the proportions of some criminal history factors were significantly different from the average in two areas. Firstly, Dorset had a low proportion of offenders aged 17-20, while its proportion with six or more previous guilty appearances was high. It would be expected that the former would tend to lower reconviction rates, and the latter to increase them. The actual reconviction rate for straight probation is, however, similar to the average. Secondly, for Oxfordshire & Buckinghamshire the proportion of offenders aged 17-20 was high, while the number who had been imprisoned while aged under 21 was low. Again, these two factors are working in opposite directions.

Similarly, for community service there was no clear relationship between the high risk factors and reconviction rates, although some of the differences in offending characteristics were reflected in these rates. For example, for Lincolnshire the proportion of offenders with six or more previous guilty appearances was high, as was the rate of acquiring previous convictions. These factors would both tend to increase reconviction rates, and indeed the rate for Lincolnshire was higher than average. For NE London, with the lowest reconviction rate for community service, three of the risk factors were low: the proportion aged 17-20, the number of previous appearances and the previous appearance rate.

In summary, therefore, there appeared to be no consistent relationships between the social characteristics and differences in reconviction rates across areas, even taking into account differences in the coding of social factors.

To examine how the area differences that were found were mirrored in the predictions made by the models, Table 6.1 gives actual and predicted reconviction rates for the separate area models for the two disposal groups discussed here. Predicted values that are significantly different from the actual values are marked with an asterisk. For straight probation (Table 6.1a) both predicted rates differ significantly from the actual for NE London, the predicted rates being lower than the actual. Adding social variables improves or maintains the predicted percentage for each area except Oxfordshire & Buckinghamshire, where the predicted rate including social variables differs significantly from the actual rate. This may be because the level of employment problems recorded in Oxfordshire & Buckinghamshire is much higher for straight probation than for community service. Adding employment as a variable therefore improves the predicted rates for the area overall, but increases the predicted rates too far for straight probation.

Table 6.1 Actual and predicted reconviction by area and disposal

a. Straight probation

	Cheshire	Dorset	Lincs	Notts	Oxon & Bucks	NE London	All six areas
Actual	62.9	54.1	53.3	48.8	47.2	52.2	52.7
Predicted (criminal History variables only)	62.1	52.2	52.6	47.6	49.3	47.1*	51.3*
Predicted (criminal History + social variables)	62.7	54.3	53.2	48.5	51.0*	48.2*	52.4
n	501	281	199	815	381	535	2,712

b. Community service

	Cheshire	Dorset	Lincs	Notts	Oxon & Bucks	NE London	All six areas
Actual	48.0	41.1	46.1	43.8	43.5	33.9	42.7
Predicted (criminal History variables only)	49.4	42.5	48.6*	45.1	44.1	38.3*	44.6*
Predicted (criminal history + social variables)	48.9	41.0	48.2*	44.1	43.0	37.1*	43.7*
n	656	387	425	799	660	664	3,591

*Significantly different from actual rate.

In Table 6.1b, for community service, both predicted rates are significantly different from the actual for Lincolnshire and NE London. However, for NE London the predicted rates are the lowest for any area, as is the actual rate, and for Lincolnshire the predicted rates, like the actual rates, are the second highest. Adding social variables improves or maintains the level of prediction in all six areas.

Implications for predicting reconviction

What implications do these results have for predicting reconviction? Clearly there are some area differences, as there are differences by disposal, which could affect reconviction. Again, logistic regression analysis has been used to test the effect of adding an area factor to the model that includes the criminal history, social and disposal group variables. Table 6.2 shows the effect of including an area factor, and summarises results from the models created by the accumulation of variable groups.

Table 6.2   The cumulative effect of groups of variables on the prediction of reconviction rates for all six areas

Model	Percentage predicted correctly	Percentage of false negatives	Improvement measure	Significant factors
Criminal history only	71.6	13.6	-	
Adding social variables	72.1	13.4	57.1	(as in Table 5.1)
Adding disposal	72.0	13.6	51.5	Community service
Adding area	72.1	13.7	54.1	Cheshire (+) Nottinghamshire (-)

The table shows that all the variables considered – criminal history variables, social variables and disposal group – do not account for all of the differences between areas. The average reconviction rate for Cheshire is higher than expected, and that for Nottinghamshire is lower. One possibility is that the remaining difference is a consequence of variation on other social factors, such as peer pressure, problems with relationships and victimisation, about which none of the areas held information. Alternatively, or in addition, other factors such as local police clear-up rates, or the availability of probation programmes in different areas, may affect reconviction differently.

7 Conclusions

This study is the first large-scale British study to consider the contribution that the social variables collected by probation services can make to the prediction of reconviction. Using retrospective data supplied by areas has provided a unique source of information about the link between social variables and reconviction. The patterns of relationships between the criminal history variables and reconviction largely match those given by Lloyd et al (1994). The data therefore provide a suitable starting point from which to examine the effects of the social variables.

Several social variables have been shown to be associated individually with reconviction, and those common to all six study areas added to the predictive power of criminal history variables in the separate area analyses. Although the effect of their addition is quite slight it is nevertheless significant, and, with consistent coding and recording of social variables across areas, it is likely that the effect on prediction would be more pronounced.

The potential improvement in prediction is greatest for those with a short criminal history and also for groups of problematic offenders, for example drugs users, the homeless and those with multiple problems. However, it will not be possible to recommend detailed changes to OGRS and performance indicators to incorporate social factors until more consistent data are available. A new study being carried out for the Home Office into the way the factors recorded in LSI-R and ACE assessments are related to reconviction should assist in this process. That study will also provide information about the link between reconviction and other dynamic social variables such as peer group pressure, problems with relationships, literacy and learning. Incorporating these and other social variables into prediction could help to confirm notions of the factors that need to be tackled to reduce reoffending, that is, ones that are criminogenic.

The current analysis has also shown that social factors affect the choice of disposal. More consistent information on these factors could be used to ensure that sentencing proposals in pre-sentence reports are better targeted and that relevant social problems are brought to sentencers' attention. Such information could also be used in future studies to check for sentencing consistency across areas and between different groups, for example by race or sex.

Work is in hand to procure a single basic risk/needs assessment tool for the probation and prison services. This will facilitate the collection of consistent national information on dynamic social factors for incorporation into risk prediction and for measuring change during supervision. It is intended that the assessment tool will be compatible with the computerised probation case recording system (known as CRAMS). This will ensure that information on social factors is recorded consistently and is easily available to probation supervisors, pre-sentence report writers and those involved in measuring the success of probation interventions at a local and national level.

At first sight it would seem logical that the coding of any variables used for prediction should be objective, to ensure consistency and comparability across and within probation areas (and prison establishments). But it is recognised that in the case of social variables a more subjective element must be included. For example, an offender's type of accommodation may not in itself affect offending behaviour; however, a perceived problem with accommodation, whatever that accommodation is, may affect offending. The same applies to factors such as employment. In this study each of the areas coded factors with a mixture of objective information and subjective assessment. Cheshire coded many variables as 'significant issues for offending', rating them as disabling, serious or moderate. In Dorset a judgement was made in the form, 'Does the problem contribute to or influence the offending behaviour?'. Similarly, in Lincolnshire the question was, 'Does the pre-sentence report explicitly state that the following are problems?'. In Oxfordshire and Buckinghamshire the coding of factors was related to their effect on offending. In Nottinghamshire substance misuse was similarly coded. In NE London the social variables were described as 'offending factors'.

A natural conclusion of the current study is that any future assessment tool should explicitly record both the objective and subjective elements of social problems. Also, as a minimum, information on dynamic social factors should be collected at the start of an order *and* at its termination. In this way the effects of the sentence can be better traced, and more accurate predictors developed. In this study there was only limited information on changes in factors, but what was available suggested a general move during supervision into more settled accommodation and into employment. It is important that this finding is validated by further research.

Despite the limitations of reconviction rates as a measure of further offending, reconviction prediction is a useful and now widely accepted method of comparing the impact of different sentences, particularly custody and community penalties. For this reason the collection of social data on prisoners should be aligned as far as possible with that collected for those serving community penalties.

Appendix A
Details of the social variables available for each area

Variable	Cheshire	Dorset	Lincoln-shire	Notts	Oxon & Bucks	NE London
Accommodation	AB	A	AF	A	AJ	A
Employment	BC	A	AF	A	AJ	AL
Alcohol	BC	E	F	AM	I	AL
Drugs	BC	E	F	AM	I	AL
Finance	BC	A	F	A	I	L
Relationships	BC	E	F	A	I	
Social skills	BC					
Literacy	BC	E		A		
Gambling				A		A
Mental health	BC	E		A	I	A
Physical health	BC	E		A		A
Ethnicity	D	D	D	D	D	D
Marital status/children		A				
Victim of physical abuse or violence		E		A		
Peer group			F			L
Aggression			F			
Other		H		GK		K

A   Detailed local code

B   Recorded at report stage as 'disabling', 'serious' or 'moderate' and described as 'significant issues for offenders'

C   Recorded at supervision stage as in note B, separately for current, previous and first.

D   Home Office code including race and ethnic origin.

E   Recorded at report stage. 'Does the problem contribute to or influence the offending behaviour?'.

F   'Does the PSR explicitly state that the following are problems?'

G   Support, community links, living arrangements.

H   Sexual problems, victim of sexual abuse, driving.

I   Problems relating to offending at start of order.

J   Recorded at start and end.

K   Other substance misuse.

L   'Offending factors'.

M   Both the need for help, and whether related to offending.

Appendix B
Details of the logistic regressions

Table B.1 *Detailed results of the logistic regressions for each area separately and for all six areas together, without social variables*

Area	Significant variables	Coeff-icient[14]	Wald statistic
Cheshire	Increasing rate of previous guilty appearances	0.073	168.39
	Type of offence[15]		22.85
	Increasing age	-0.044	18.98
	Group 8 (aged 17-20, 1 previous)	0.782	6.71
	Group A (aged 28+, 0-1 previous)	-0.857	4.86
	Group 22 (aged 17-21, 6-11 previous)	0.955	4.57
	Constant	-2.252	30.64
Dorset	Increasing rate of previous guilty appearances	0.063	91.29
	Group A (aged 28+, 0-1 previous)	-1.32	13.44
	Constant	-3.01	81.20
Lincolnshire	Increasing rate of previous guilty appearances	0.050	69.07
	Increasing age	-0.056	26.26
	Group 4 (aged 21-27, no previous)	-1.455	7.01
	Group C (aged 24-29, 5-9 previous)	-0.697	4.60
	Group 18 (aged 22-23, 3-5 previous)	-0.901	4.50
	Constant	-0.866	3.86

14 Each variable in this table (and the others in this appendix) had 1 degree of freedom, except offence, which had 9.
15 No individual offence reached significance.

Table B.1 continued

Area	Significant variables	Coeff-icient	Wald statistic
Nottinghamshire	Increasing rate of previous guilty appearances	0.058	105.08
	Previous adult custody	0.211	13.97
	Group 19 (aged 21, 3-5 previous)	1.376	12.20
	Group 20 (aged 17-20, 3-5 previous)	0.720	11.36
	Group 9 (aged 17-20, 2 previous)	0.895	9.98
	Group 21 (aged 22-23, 6-11 previous)	0.994	8.47
	Group 22 (aged 17-21, 6-11 previous)	0.679	5.84
	Increasing age	-0.022	4.83
	Group 8 (aged 17-20, 1 previous)	0.547	4.77
	Constant	-2.814	44.52
Oxfordshire & Buckinghamshire	Increasing rate of previous guilty appearances	0.054	110.96
	Increasing age	-0.075	51.34
	Previous adult custody	0.119	4.73
	Constant	-0.900	5.38
NE London	Increasing rate of previous guilty appearances	0.074	203.70
	Increasing age	-0.039	21.56
	Group 10 (aged 30+, 3-5 previous)	0.912	10.67
	Constant	-2.754	61.26
All six areas	Increasing rate of previous guilty appearances	0.052	135.97
	Type of offence:		69.96
	burglary	0.326	
	theft & handling	0.290	
	Group A (aged 28+, 0-1 previous)	-1.105	58.06
	Group 4 (aged 21-27, no previous)	-1.078	51.16
	Increasing age	-0.041	50.23
	Group B (aged 21-27, 1-2 previous)	-0.576	33.05
	Group 7 (aged 17-20, no previous)	-0.654	22.03
	Previous adult custody	0.127	19.56
	Group 12 (aged 24-29, 3-4 previous)	-0.477	14.00
	Previous guilty appearances	-0.035	7.99
	Group 23 (aged 17-23, 12+ previous)	0.978	6.61
	Group C (aged 24-29, 5-9 previous)	-0.216	4.74
	Group 3 (aged 28+, 2 previous)	-0.368	4.57
	Group 22 (aged 17-21, 6-11 previous)	0.297	4.25
	Constant	-1.245	16.44

Table B.2   Detailed results of the logistic regressions for each area separately and fall six areas together, with social variables

Area	Significant variables	Coeff-icient	Wald statistic
Cheshire	Increasing rate of previous guilty appearances	0.071	153.07
	Type of offence[16]		19.72
	Increasing age	-0.043	17.40
	Group 8 (aged 17-20, 1 previous)	0.782	6.68
	Group A (aged 28+, 0-1 previous)	-0.868	4.99
	Drugs	0.462	4.89
	Group 22 (aged 17-21, 6-11 previous)	0.977	4.77
	Constant	-2.220	29.72
Dorset	Increasing rate of previous guilty appearances	0.061	83.44
	Group A (aged 28+, 0-1 previous)	-1.384	14.29
	Drugs*employment	1.123	9.57
	Alcohol*employment*finances	1.146	4.68
	Constant	-3.004	79.21
Lincolnshire	Increasing rate of previous guilty appearances	0.048	65.53
	Increasing age	-0.055	25.47
	Group 4 (aged 21-27, no previous)	-1.421	6.69
	Drugs*employment	0.936	6.19
	Group C (aged 24-29, 5-9 previous)	-0.708	4.72
	Group 18 (aged 22-23, 3-5 previous)	-0.922	4.59
	Constant	-0.877	3.92
Nottinghamshire	Increasing rate of previous guilty appearances	0.056	92.50
	Previous adult custody	0.204	12.98
	Group 19 (aged 21, 3-5 previous)	1.355	11.83
	Group 20 (aged 17-20, 3-5 previous)	0.715	11.02
	Group 9 (aged 17-20, 2 previous)	0.914	10.27
	Finances	0.402	9.80
	Group 21 (aged 22-23, 6-11 previous)	1.006	8.55
	Accommodation	0.421	7.43
	Group 22 (aged 17-21, 6-11 previous)	0.685	5.88
	Group 8 (aged 17-20, 1 previous)	0.561	4.94
	Increasing age	-0.021	4.52
	Constant	-3.044	50.23

16   No individual ofence reached significance.

Table B.2 continued

Area	Significant variables	Coefficient	Wald statistic
Oxfordshire & Buckinghamshire	Increasing rate of previous guilty appearances	0.053	98.17
	Increasing age	-0.076	50.72
	Drugs*employment	0.809	15.63
	Employment*finances	0.450	10.74
	Group 13 (aged 24-29, 5-9 previous, no financial problems)	-0.637	4.94
	Previous adult custody	0.121	4.83
	Constant	-0.987	6.19
NE London	Increasing rate of previous guilty appearances	0.065	142.07
	Drugs	1.095	26.05
	Increasing age	-0.037	17.81
	Group 5 (aged 21-27, 1-2 previous, no employment problems)	-0.717	7.28
	Group 10 (aged 30+, 3-5 previous)	0.703	5.94
	Group 1 (aged 28+, 0-1 previous, no financial problems)	-0.776	5.42
	Alcohol*drugs	-0.896	4.37
	Constant	-2.393	42.61
All six areas	Increasing rate of previous guilty appearances	0.052	129.77
	Type of offence:		58.20
	burglary	0.288	
	theft & handling	0.224	
	Group 4 (aged 21-27, no previous)	-1.066	49.83
	Increasing age	-0.041	49.08
	Group B (aged 21-27, 1-2 previous)	-0.580	33.21
	Drugs	0.659	31.68
	Alcohol*drugs	-0.687	23.93
	Group 7 (aged 17-20, no previous)	-0.657	22.07
	Previous adult custody	0.131	20.59
	Group 12 (aged 24-29, 3-4 previous)	-0.453	12.51
	Accommodation*alcohol*drugs*employment	0.736	12.40
	Group A (aged 28+, 0-1 previous)	-0.695	12.18
	Previous guilty appearances	-0.041	10.39
	Group C (aged 24-29, 5-9 previous)	-0.370	9.18
	Group 1 (aged 28+, 0-1 previous, no financial problems)	-0.649	7.25
	Group 23 (aged 17-23, 12+ previous)	1.020	7.16
	Group 14 (aged 24-29, 5-9 previous, financial problems)	0.452	5.41
	Group 22 (aged 17-21, 6-11 previous)	0.328	5.15
	Group 16 (aged 28+, 10+ previous, drugs problem)	0.440	4.44
	Group 3 (aged 28+, 2 previous)	-0.356	4.27
	Constant	-1.215	15.51

Table B.3   ***Detailed results of the logistic regressions for each area separately and for all six areas together, with social variables and disposal***

Area	Significant variables	Coeff-icient	Wald statistic
NE London	Increasing rate of previous guilty appearances	0.0624	130.83
	Drugs	0.984	20.34
	Increasing age	-0.040	19.64
	Community service	-0.375	8.10
	Group 5 (aged 21-27, 1-2 previous, no employment problems)	-0.727	7.45
	Group 1 (aged 28+, 0-1 previous, no financial problems)	-0.786	5.54
	Group 10 (aged 30+, 3-5 previous)	0.674	5.43
	Alcohol*drugs	-0.898	4.38
	Constant	-2.035	27.64
All six areas	Increasing rate of previous guilty appearances	0.050	123.36
	Type of offence:		58.16
	burglary	0.284	
	theft & handling	0.215	
	Group 4 (aged 21-27, no previous)	-1.057	48.84
	Increasing age	-0.042	50.42
	Group B (aged 21-27, 1-2 previous)	-0.579	33.00
	Drugs	0.620	27.58
	Alcohol*drugs	-0.669	22.63
	Group 7 (aged 17-20, no previous)	-0.657	22.09
	Previous adult custody	0.129	20.00
	Group 12 (aged 24-29, 3-4 previous)	-0.451	12.43
	Group A (aged 28+, 0-1 previous)	-0.701	12.38
	Accommodation*alcohol*drugs*employment	0.719	11.85
	Previous guilty appearances	-0.040	9.57
	Group C (aged 24-29, 5-9 previous)	-0.374	9.37
	Group 23 (aged 17-23, 12+ previous)	1.017	7.12
	Group 1 (aged 28+, 0-1 previous, no financial problems)	-0.640	7.05
	Community service	-0.135	6.01
	Group 14 (aged 24-29, 5-9 previous, financial problems)	0.454	5.46
	Group 22 (aged 17-21, 6-11 previous)	0.329	5.19
	Group 3 (aged 28+, 2 previous)	-0.366	4.51
	Group 16 (aged 28+, 10+ previous, drugs problem)	0.436	4.35
	Constant	-1.077	11.78

Note: Disposal was not significant for the other areas

Table B.4 **Detailed results of the logistic regressions for all six areas together, with social variables, disposal and area**

Area	Significant variables	Coeff-icient	Wald statistic
All six areas	Increasing rate of previous guilty appearances	0.050	119.30
	Type of offence:		60.99
	sexual	-0.236	
	burglary	0.292	
	theft & handling	0.230	
	Group 4 (aged 21-27, no previous)	-1.073	50.11
	Increasing age	-0.042	51.67
	Group B (aged 21-27, 1-2 previous)	-0.571	32.05
	Group 7 (aged 17-20, no previous)	-0.678	23.31
	Drugs	0.556	21.64
	Previous adult custody	0.129	19.98
	Cheshire	0.281	14.58
	Group 12 (aged 24-29, 3-4 previous)	-0.453	12.50
	Group A (aged 28+, 0-1 previous)	-0.663	11.03
	Group C (aged 24-29, 5-9 previous)	-0.406	10.91
	Accommodation*alcohol*drugs*employment	0.689	10.82
	Previous guilty appearances	-0.038	8.90
	Alcohol*drugs	-0.445	8.48
	Group 1 (aged 28+, 0-1 previous, no financial problems)	-0.693	8.24
	Group 14 (aged 24-29, 5-9 previous, financial problems)	0.553	7.93
	Group 23 (aged 17-23, 12+ previous)	1.006	6.93
	Nottinghamshire	-0.195	6.90
	Community service	-0.135	5.99
	Group 22 (aged 17-21, 6-11 previous)	0.331	5.24
	Group 3 (aged 28+, 2 previous)	-0.379	4.80
	Group 16 (aged 28+, 10+ previous, drugs problem)	0.457	4.76
	Constant	-1.054	11.12

Appendix C
Interaction groups

Table C.1   Interactions between variables affecting reconviction rate

Group number	Previous guilty appearances	Age	Reconviction rate %	n	Other factor
1	0 or 1	28 or more	8.6	512	No financial problems
2	0 or 1	28 or more	16.9	231	Financial problems
3	2	28 or more	21.5	260	
4	0	21 to 27	19.5	380	
5	1 or 2	21 to 27	29.6	395	No employment problems
6	1 or 2	21 to 27	39.2	278	Employment problems
7	0	17 to 20	31.2	391	
8	1 or 2	17 to 20	55.2	373	
9	1 or 2	17 to 20	65.5	287	
10	3 to 5	30 or more	26.2	386	
11	6 to 9	30 or more	39.9	326	
12	3 or 4	24 to 29	37.7	316	
13	5 to 9	24 to 29	50.2	317	No financial problems
14	5 to 9	24 to 29	61.5	187	Financial problems
15	10 or more	28 or more	56.7	541	No drug problem
16	10 or more	28 or more	73.7	175	Drug problem
17	10 or more	24 to 27	78.0	346	
18	3 to 5	22 to 23	56.6	265	
19	3 to 5	21	67.5	151	
20	3 to 5	17 to 20	75.6	516	
21	6 to 11	22 to 23	74.3	257	
22	6 to 11	17 to 21	83.3	437	
23	12 or more	17 to 23	93.0	114	

Group number	Previous guilty appearances	Age	Reconviction rate %	n	Parent of groups:
A	0 or 1	28 or more	11.2	743	1, 2
B	1 or 2	21 to 27	33.6	673	5, 6
C	5 to 9	24 to 29	54.4	504	13, 14
D	10 or more	28 or more	60.9	716	15, 16

Table C.2 Interactions between variables associated with Community Service as the choice of disposal

Group number	Percent-age CSO	n	Sex	Age	Social problems	Previous guilty appearances	Youth custody	High risk offence?
1	11	198	F		Substance misuse			
2	18	319	M		Accommodation & substance misuse	5 or more		
3	22	386	M		Substance misuse	5 or more		Yes
7	23	278	F		Financial			
9	27	184	M		Accommodation		Yes	
5	28	262	M		Accommodation & substance misuse	0 to 4		
4	35	482	M		Substance misuse	5 or more		No
8	41	262	F		None			
6	42	786	M		Substance misuse	0 to 4		
10	46	505	M		Accommodation		No	
11	52	775	M	17 to 23	Employment			
13	54	269	M		Financial			
14	60	291	M		None	10 or more		
12	60	700	M	24 or more	Employment			
15	66	589	M	17 to 25	None	2 to 9		
16	76	421	M	26 or more	None	2 to 9		
17	77	734	M		None	0 or 1		
All	48	7,441						

References

Andrews, D. and Bonta, J. (1995). *LSI-R: The Level of Service Inventory – Revised.* Toronto: Multi-Health Systems Inc.

Aubrey, R. and Hough, M. (1997). *Assessing Offenders' Needs: Assessment Scales for the Probation Service.* Home Office Research Study No 166. London: Home Office.

Burnett, R. (1994). 'The Odds of Going Straight: Offenders' Own Predictions', in *Sentencing and Risk: Proceedings of the 10th Annual Conference on Research and Information in the Probation Service.* Birmingham: Midlands Probation Training Consortium.

Burnett, R. (1996). *Fitting Supervision to Offenders: Assessment and Allocation Decisions in the Probation Service.* Home Office Research Study No 153. London: Home Office.

Copas, J. B.(1998). *The Offending Group Reconviction Scale: a Statistical Reconviction Score for Use by Probation Officers.* Applied Statistics, Volume 47, Part 1.

Copas, J. B., Marshall, P. and Tarling, R. (1996). *Predicting Reoffending for Discretionary Conditional Release.* Home Office Research Study No 150. London: Home Office.

Dowds, L. and Hedderman, C. (1997). 'The sentencing of men and women', in *Understanding the sentencing of women,* (eds) Hedderman, C. and Gelsthorpe, L. Home Office Research Study No 170. London: Home Office.

Edmunds, M., May, T., Hearnden, I. and Hough, M. (1998) *Arrest Referral: Emerging Lessons from the Research.* Drug Prevention Initiative Paper 23. London: Home Office.

Goldblatt, P. and Lewis, C. (eds) (1998) *Reducing offending: an assessment of research evidence on ways of dealing with offending behaviour.* Home Office Research Study No 187. London: Home Office.

HMI Probation (1995) *Dealing with Dangerous People: the probation service and public protection.* Report of a Thematic Inspection. London: Home Office.

Home Office/ACOP (1997) *Management and Assessment of Risk in the Probation Service.* London: Home Office.

Humphrey, C., Carter, P. and Pease, K. (1992) 'A Reconviction Predictor for Probationers'. *British Journal of Social Work, 22.*

Kemshall, H. (1996). *Reviewing Risk. A Review of Research on the Assessment and Management of Risk and Dangerousness: Implications for Policy and Practice in the Probation Service.* London: Home Office Research and Statistics Directorate.

Kershaw, C. (1997). *Reconvictions of those commencing Community Penalties in 1993, England and Wales.* Home Office Statistical Bulletin 6/97. London: Home Office Research and Statistics Directorate.

Lloyd, C., Mair, G. and Hough, M. (1994). *Explaining Reconviction Rates: A Critical Analysis.* Home Office Research Study No 136. London: Home Office.

Merrington, S. (1990). *The Cambridgeshire Risk of Reconviction Scale.* Cambridgeshire Probation Service.

Nuttall, C. P. with Barnard, E. E., Fowles, A. J., Frost, A., Hammond, W. H., Mayhew, P., Pease, K., Tarling, R. and Weatheritt, M. J. (1977). *Parole in England and Wales.* Home Office Research Study No 38. London: HMSO.

Oldfield, M. (1996). *The Kent Reconviction Survey.* Kent Probation Service.

Sutton, D. and Davies, P. (1996). *An Introduction to the "Level of Service Inventory – Revised" (LSI-R).* Cardiff: Cognitive Centre Foundation.

Ward, D. (1987). *The Validity of the Reconviction Prediction Score.* Home Office Research Study No 94. London: HMSO.

Publications

List of research publications

The most recent research reports published are listed below. A **full** list of publications is available on request from the Research, Development and Statistics Directorate, Information and Publications Group.

Home Office Research Studies (HORS)

183. **Drugs and crime: the results of research on drug testing and interviewing arrestees.** Trevor Bennett. 1998.

184. **Remand decisions and offending on bail: evaluation of the Bail Process Project.** Patricia M Morgan and Paul F Henderson. 1998.

185. **Entry into the criminal justice system: a survey of police arrests and their outcomes.** Coretta Phillips and David Brown with the assistance of Zoë James and Paul Goodrich. 1998

186. **The restricted hospital order: from court to the community.** Robert Street. 1998

187. **Reducing Offending: An assessment of research evidence on ways of dealing with offending behaviour.** Edited by Peter Goldblatt and Chris Lewis. 1998.

188. **Lay visiting to police stations.** Mollie Weatheritt and Carole Vieira. 1998

189. **Mandatory drug testing in prisons: The relationship between MDT and the level and nature of drug misuse.** Kimmett Edgar and Ian O'Donnell. 1998

190. **Trespass and protest: policing under the Criminal Justice and Public Order Act 1994.** Tom Bucke and Zoë James. 1998.

191. **Domestic Violence: Findings from a new British Crime Survey self-completion questionnaire.** Catriona Mirrlees-Black. 1999.

Research Findings

63. **Neighbourhood watch co-ordinators.** Elizabeth Turner and Banos Alexandrou. 1997.

64. **Attitudes to punishment: findings from the 1996 British Crime Survey.** Michael Hough and Julian Roberts. 1998.

65. **The effects of video violence on young offenders.** Kevin Browne and Amanda Pennell. 1998.

66. **Electronic monitoring of curfew orders: the second year of the trials.** Ed Mortimer and Chris May. 1998.

67. **Public perceptions of drug-related crime in 1997.** Nigel Charles. 1998.

68. **Witness care in magistrates' courts and the youth court.** Joyce Plotnikoff and Richard Woolfson. 1998.

69. **Handling stolen goods and theft: a market reduction approach.** Mike Sutton. 1998.

70. **Drug testing arrestees.** Trevor Bennett. 1998.

71. **Prevention of plastic card fraud.** Michael Levi and Jim Handley. 1998.

72. **Offending on bail and police use of conditional bail.** David Brown. 1998.

73. **Voluntary after-care.** Mike Maguire, Peter Raynor, Maurice Vanstone and Jocelyn Kynch. 1998.

74. **Fast-tracking of persistent young offenders.** John Graham. 1998.

75. **Mandatory drug testing in prisons – an evaluation.** Kimmett Edgar and Ian O'Donnell. 1998.

76. **The prison population in 1997: a statistical review.** Philip White. 1998.

77. **Rural areas and crime: findings from the British crime survey.** Catriona Mirrlees-Black. 1998.

78. **A review of classification systems for sex offenders.** Dawn Fisher and George Mair. 1998.

79. **An evaluation of the prison sex offender treatment programme.** Anthony Beech et al. 1998.

80. **Age limits for babies in prison: some lessons from abroad.** Diane Caddle. 1998.

81. **Motor projects in England & Wales: an evaluation.** Darren Sugg. 1998

82. **HIV/Aids risk behaviour among adult male prisoners.** John Strange et al. 1998.

83. **Concern about crime: findings from the 1998 British Crime Survey.** Catriona Mirrlees-Black and Jonathan Allen. 1998.

84. **Transfers from prison to hospital - the operation of section 48 of the Mental Health Act 1983.** Ronnie Mackay and David Machin. 1998.

85. **Evolving crack cocaine careers.** Kevin Brain, Howard Parker and Tim Bottomley. 1998.

86. **Domestic Violence: Findings from the BCS self-completion questionnaire.** 1999. Catriona Mirrlees-Black and Carole Byron. 1999.

Occasional Papers

The impact of the national lottery on the horse-race betting levy. Simon Field and James Dunmore. 1997.

The cost of fires. A review of the information available. Donald Roy. 1997.

Monitoring and evaluation of WOLDS remand prison and comparisons with public-sector prisons, in particular HMP Woodhill. A Keith Bottomley, Adrian James, Emma Clare and Alison Liebling. 1997.

Evaluation of the 'One Stop Shop' and victim statement pilot projects. Carolyn Hoyle, Ed Cape, Rod Morgan and Andrew Sanders. 1998.

Requests for Publications

Home Office Research Studies, Research Findings and *Occasional Papers* can be requested from:

Research, Development and Statistics Directorate
Information and Publications Group
Room 201, Home Office
50 Queen Anne's Gate
London SW1H 9AT
Telephone: 0171-273 2084
Facsimile: 0171-222 0211
Internet: http://www.homeoffice.gov.uk/rds/index.htm
E-mail: rds.ho@gtnet.gov.uk